S0-AJX-572

THE
TELLURIDE
S·T·O·R·Y

BY DAVID LAVENDER → WITH PHOTOGRAPHY BY GEORGE H. H. HUEY

Wayfinder PRESS

Published by Wayfinder Press, P. O. Box 217, Ridgway, Colorado 81432

Editor: Jack Swanson
Designer: Christina Watkins
Color Photography: George H. H. Huey
Copy Editing: Rose Houk
Typography: Typesmith, Inc., Tucson, Arizona
Lithography: Pyramid Printing, Grand Junction, Colorado
Text © 1987 by David Lavender
Color photography © by George H. H. Huey
All rights reserved including the right of reproduction in whole or in part.

ISBN 0-9608764-6-4

CONTENTS

Perhaps this unidentified couple are honeymooners headed for a new home. Perhaps they have luxurious camping in mind. Anyway, life is clearly good, even without automobiles. Denver Public Library Western History Department

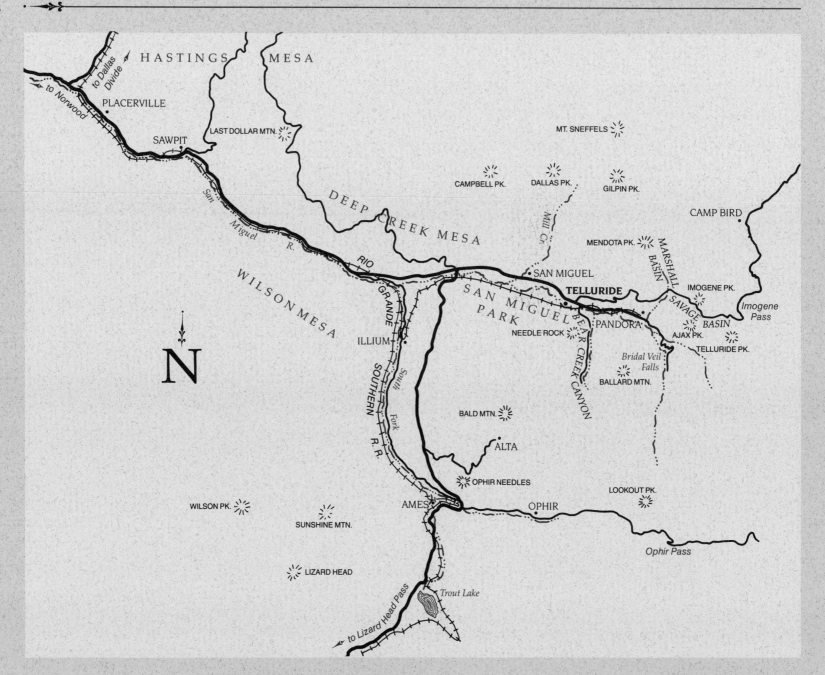

PREFACE

A knowledge of history is able to make the whole
landscape alive, to render the exploration of
the humblest village an adventure of thrilling
possibilities, to give a voice to the downs,
and to enrich the waste with memories.

—Wingfield-Stratford by way of
Robert Glass Cleland

In the pages that follow I have sought to restore voices to those builders of Telluride who are drifting into silence, overpowered by the hurly-burly clang of changes they could not possibly have foreseen. And to give a voice to the town itself, where I was born and spent much of my boyhood. To a town that didn't even settle firmly on a name during the first half dozen years or so of its life. To the town that became the staging area for the platoons of ragged prospectors who tested and tunneled the high country and afterwards provided them with relaxation, bawdy enough sometimes, when they came back to celebrate success, reinvigorate themselves for another effort, or, too often, to walk away in defeat.

"The Town Without a Bellyache" it called itself on occasion, forgetting, in those times of well-being, the industrial warfare that all but tore it apart as the twentieth century opened. But most of all I have hoped to give voice to those who toughed out the grim years after the mines had closed and before the magic of snow— plain, ordinary, death-dealing, exhilarating snow—had wrought its transformations.

It is a unique place, this born-again Telluride, and yet from its singular particulars one can draw many of the historic generalities that explain much of the energy of all Colorado. It is something to muse about as you hike trails the mule trains followed, drive jeeps over roads built for wagons, prowl around the old dumps beside the leaning, brown-weathered mine buildings, or ride ski lifts so closely related to the ore trams whose wheels clicked across their support towers a hundred years ago. Listen as you go. Listen. The voices are there.

CHAPTER ONE • **THE TOWN MAKERS**

Early June, 1878. The season's usual dry wind keened across San Miguel Park nearly 9,000 feet high in southwestern Colorado's San Juan Mountains. Springtime, almost. The ground in the Park—"park" being a generic term for almost any relatively flat, relatively open piece of earth rimmed by mountains—was bare and fresh smelling. New leaves brightened the tangles of scrub willows that grew in boggy spots downstream from a handful of new cabins that after various contretemps would be named Telluride. They misted with pale green the grove of aspens that hid the red gash where Cornet Creek (it should be spelled Cornett because it was named not for a musical instrument but for prospector W. L. Cornett) burst into the Park on its way to join the swollen San Miguel River. Springtime, though wind-whipped banners of snow still flared off the enormous horseshoe of peaktops and high ridges that cupped the Park, a dazzle of white against a sky so blue that looking at it hurt one's eyes.

Sap rising. Preparations to make. That snow could not last much longer. Soon the miners who had built some of the log cabins in the Park would start pushing up the trails to the claims they had staked out the year before, many well above timberline. Prospectors who had found no veins worth exploring would resume their searches. Placer miners farther down the river were digging ditches and hammering together flumes for carrying water to the benches of gold-flecked gravel that bordered the San Miguel River for scores of miles. Foresighted merchants whose packtrains were already jogging single-file along the trail leading up the river were joyfully passing out kerosene, coffee, dried foods—a popular saying declared that any man who would not eat beans was a son of a bitch—drill steel, shovels, picks, gads, which are a kind of crowbar, boots, gloves, chemicals for running crude assays, writing paper, dutch ovens, and anything else a man might take it into his head to order.

Through it all ran a thought that had been gathering force throughout the winter: *This camp ought to be a town.* A legally incorporated town for distributing goods, taking in valuable metals, handling currency, settling disputes, building schools, agitating for county-maintained roads and trails. Most particularly there *had* to be a post office. It wasn't just that mail service would connect this camp, located at the farthest edge of the San Juan Mountains, to the rest of the state and the nation. A post office was a giver of identity. It put a town on the map, figuratively as well as literally. By declaring stability, it would help attract outside investors almost as much as viable transportation would.

View of Telluride from north

Besides, there were rivals to be considered, one to the east and another to the west.

San Miguel Park is approximately six miles long, with a maximum width of about half a mile. Its axis tilts slightly to the north of true west. At the northwestern end, the land drops suddenly, pitching the river down a stepladder of foaming cascades to a junction with its south fork. At the top of the cascades, the Keystone Hydraulic Company was about to launch, that year of 1878, the earth-shattering operations whose heritage would be the name Keystone Hill, which is still attached to the steep grade by which the modern highway climbs into San Miguel Park. At the close of the 1870s such visiting journalists as George Crofutt and Frank Fossett were more impressed by these placer operations and by the town which was closest to them, San Miguel City, than they were by developments farther upcountry.

San Miguel City—the word "City" was, of course, a bow toward the future—was located on the north margin of the Park, two miles upstream from the top of the Keystone cascades. At that point Mill Creek drops thunderously into the Park from the blocky shoulders of Dallas Peak, 13,809 feet high. On breaking into the flatlands, the boisterous creek abruptly turns placid. In 1878 it seemed to sparkle with economic opportunities. One attraction was the amount of land and water available for ore-treating plants. In addition, wild hay grew profusely in the nearby meadows; Linnard Remine and his small party had proved this back in 1872 by scything down enough grass to feed their trail-weary packstock.

During the next few years more people, including one dauntless woman who opened a restaurant, trickled in. By the end of 1877 San Miguel City, estimated population one hundred, had been laid out. Twice-a-week mail service (horseback in summer, skis in winter) linked the new village to Silverton by way of Ophir Pass, 11,798 feet in elevation. It was a pretty place. The settlers did not attack the nearby conifers as ruthlessly as did most mining camp residents when in need of wood. An almost pastoral aspect took hold when—

novel twist in young mining camps—an enterprising farmer drove in a small herd of black-and-white dairy cows. Such a town, its citizens believed, would prove to be a serious contender if any civic rivalries cropped up in the area.

Far less pastoral was the settlement of Newport, located in a cramped open space at the Park's eastern tip. Winter shadows lay deep there. Still, the scenery was a decided plus, for the town stood almost within the spray of the three impetuous streams that united to form the San Miguel River. First, Marshall Creek, deeply canyoned, plunges in from the north. A bit farther east and across the narrowing valley from Marshall Creek, Bridal Veil Creek forms a lacy waterfall 365 feet high and then curls, jumps, and dives toward the Park among clusters of monstrous boulders fallen from the surrounding cliffs. A second waterfall, Ingram, draws a silver stream down the cliffs at the very head of the surrounding horse-shoe of cliffs.

Newport crouched in this prodigious cleft because of two mines. One was operated by Folsom and Company at a now indeterminate site in what was then called Water Fall Gulch. The other property, staked out in 1875 and hence one of the valley's earliest lode claims, was the Pandora Mine. It was located just east of the point where Marshall Creek slashed out of the high country. Young Newport, created to house the workers of both mines and their suppliers, probably took shape on the west bank of the creek, opposite the Pandora Mine. Although the site had been surveyed in 1876, the town had not been awarded a post office because there was another Newport in Colorado. Such mail as its inhabitants received arrived by special arrangement with San Miguel City.

So matters stood in the spring of 1878. Two ambitious towns hardly three miles apart already yearned to dominate the local economic and political scene. And then another contender, Telluride-to-be, appeared halfway between them.

To have true status, this new town would need to be incorporated, a step that involved dispatching an appropriate petition to the county government. (At that time San Miguel Park and, indeed, all of the river's basin lay in Ouray County, whose seat was also named Ouray.) Preparing the necessary papers under the date of January 10, 1878, the promoters had tramped through the snow from cabin to cabin and had collected thirty-three signatures, an apparently safe margin above the legal requirement of thirty. Two signers, being illiterate, made their marks; authenticity was attested to by Harry Lake, justice of the peace and also one of the town promoters, along with Edward McFarland, A. B. Cooper, G.N. Hyde, and John Eder. It need not be assumed, of course, that every signature was actually collected on January 10.

The next step was to decide on how big a townsite to ask the federal government for. Its cost, when patent was finally issued, would be $1.25 an acre. The leaders in the movement decided eighty acres—a rectangle a little more than half a mile long and a quarter of a mile wide—would be enough. These acres would have to be located by survey so precisely that anyone anywhere in the world could tell where the town was just by consulting the proper map.

It is not clear how the mapping was done. The promoters did have reference points. In the fall of 1874 a three-man unit of the Hayden Survey had gone through the country establishing triangulation stations as a first essential in preparing, for the federal government, a topographic map of the San Juan Mountains. The trio had placed its station number 32 at elevation 8,880 feet on a hillside at the western tip of San Miguel Park. Other stations had been placed on prominent peaks in the vicinity. None of the peaktop stations was visible from the proposed townsite, but usable lines had probably been run out from them for the sake of miners intent on recording their claims incontrovertibly.

Be that as it may, the town surveyor managed to set up, on February 23, what he called a government locating post. Next he placed a second post, a sturdy four-by-four, at the predetermined northeast corner of the eighty-acre rectangle. Other reference points included the river, two spruce trees twelve inches in diameter, and a large aspen. When the squinting, walking, and calculating were finished, the rectangle was portrayed, according to proper scale, on a sheet of paper. Not precisely, though, for later measurements showed that it contained only 78.57 acres. However, the drawing and its accompanying mathematical lingo would be sufficient when the time came to ask the government for an official location certificate.

The town's outlines determined, the streets were staked and named, and the whole was given graphic representation on a drawing called a plat. The name chosen for the yet unborn town was Columbia, hardly a striking designation in view of the numerous Columbias and Columbuses already scattered around the nation. The time would come when there would be second thinking about that name.

Though the site's median elevation was just under 8,800 feet, it was sheltered by high mountains and should be fairly comfortable. The river ran at the base of the steep, heavily forested south side of the Park. That was where the cold shadows would fall during winter. The town itself, however, lay on the gentle, south-facing north slope and would catch the winter sunshine. The surveyed area was marred neither by bogs nor hazardous gullies. Though the red hillside at the town's northern edge steepened quickly, there was no catchment basin immediately above the site to collect snow, and hence there would be slight danger from avalanches, an advantage Newport did not have.

There was considerable danger from snow elsewhere, however, and no one was anxious to carry the petition and maps through the untracked drifts to Ouray. Time slipped by, the tiny new leaves on the willows showed tinges of red and then turned green, and suddenly June was at hand. Time to move. Whereupon glitches developed. Three of the people who had signed the petition in January were in the mountains, prospecting, though the law required them to be in residence at the time the county received the papers. And suppose the county officials declared one or more of the signatures invalid.

Miner's cabin, Telluride

To make sure the legal minimum of thirty persons was on hand, the promoters sent messengers scrambling after the missing trio. Meanwhile Justice of the Peace Harry Lake took testimony from the town's (and his) lawyer, J. P. Cassidy, who stated he knew for a fact the three absentees would be in town by the time the petition reached Ouray.

That done, the papers were put in Cassidy's hands and he was told to make tracks for Ouray. Possibly he climbed the steep zigzags of Marshall Creek to Imogene Pass, 13,000 feet high, and then followed Canyon Creek to Ouray, a vertical drop of more than a mile. Lingering snow and high water, however, may have persuaded him to take the longer, low-country route instead—perhaps the same Indian trail around Last Dollar Mountain and across Hastings Mesa that Linnard Remine's party had followed into the area in 1872. Anyway, he reached Ouray in time for the petition to be filed on June 8.

Judge Theron Stevens ordered an election on the matter for July 13, 1878, to make sure that the majority of residents really wanted a town with its taxes and legalisms, regardless of what the petition said. Should the vote be affirmative, Harry Lake, Edward McFarland, A. B. Cooper, and John Eder were to be the town commissioners. Because G. N. Hyde, another of the original promoters, had vanished he was replaced by John Donnellan, an energetic prospector of whom we will hear more.

Notices of the election were posted, as required by law, on trees and cabins in eight different places. Forty-six qualified voters were registered. On the assigned day, however, only twenty-eight showed up at the polling place, George Tuttle's cabin. (The rest were probably out combing the summer-bright mountains.) Incorporation won unanimously. Columbia, Colorado, was now a legal entity. No post office yet. Still, the incorporators could look back on the past with satisfaction and ahead to the future with optimism.

CHAPTER TWO · **THE OUTER EDGE**

As far as I am aware, no one has yet calculated how many billions of dollars, adjusted for inflation, have been dug out of the Colorado Mineral Belt, a broad zone of crustal deformation that creases the heart of the Rockies diagonally from the vicinity of Boulder southwest to the heavily glaciated dome of the San Juan Mountains. Within the long Belt are many apparently random concentrations of fissures through which hot mineral juices long ago oozed up toward the surface. Cooled, the solutions and the country rock with which they were mixed became ore, rich, some-times, in gold, silver, lead, and zinc. The only significant Colorado mining region that lies outside this most fortuitous diagonal is the Cripple Creek area on the western slope of Pikes Peak.

It is possible to trace the geologic history of the San Juan Mountains, the Belt's southwestern extremity, for considerably more than a billion years. For our purposes here, however, it is enough to start with the dome as it existed some thirty-five million years ago. Though lofty when the Rockies were first uplifted during the Laramide Revolution some seventy million years ago, the bulge had probably been reduced by erosion to a minor, rolling swell. But times change. Deep-seated tectonic forces pushed the land up again, and throughout the entire region (except for the Needle Mountains south of today's Silverton), volcanoes exploded on and off for about seven million years. Several of the fiery monsters blew out their own hearts. Their unsupported tops and walls collapsed to form giant calderas whose outlines are discernible now only to trained geologists.

Easier to differentiate, in places, are the generally horizontal layers of volcanic tuffs, breccias, and occasional lavas that were laid down by the successive eruptions. The layers average 1,500 feet in depth; some accumulations are nearly three times that. It was from these discharges that the San Juan high country received its characteristic gray hue. Meanwhile magma, threaded erratically with molten ores, had welled up into the yawning calderas, creating secondary mountains, and into the adjacent fissures. Sometimes the material spilled over; sometimes it came to rest internally, to be exposed later by erosion. When the minerals in the compounds, principally widely diffused specks of iron, were oxidized by contact with the air, flamboyant streaks and patches of red and yellow appeared, vivid contrasts to the light green of the alpine tundra and the darker green of the forests on the lower slopes.

The moment the mountains raised their heads they were attacked by erosion—water, wind-borne sand at times, chemical reactions, and physical disintegration caused by freezing moisture, expanding tree roots, and the ceaseless burrowing of an infinite number of insects and animals. The greatest carver, however, was glacial ice, compacted out of the huge accumulations of snow that gathered in the high country during four different eras when world temperatures dropped and vast ice sheets advanced out of the north. The San Juans were not in the path of the major ice flows, but they were lofty enough to create, in the frigid temperatures that surrounded them, their own glacial caps. Gravity pulled these caps downward along existing streambeds. The ice, studded with sharp-edged boulders, scoured the soft volcanic tuff into magnificent shapes. It honed gentle ridges into knife-edged arêtes, scooped handsome cirques into the sides of the more massive peaks, and whittled others into horns. Retreating at last, it left behind deep, U-shaped troughs boxed in at their upper ends by soaring headwalls.

A story-book example of these glacial gouges is the high-walled, flat-bottomed trough that contains San Miguel Park, with waterfalls and cascades pouring into it from hanging valleys on either side. The mess of clastic rock produced by so much destruction was washed down into the San Miguel's red, white, and tan canyons, their walls clearly showing the sedimentary layers deposited in the ancient seas that had glistened there long before the uplifting of the Rockies. In many places those gravel beds, which reach more than sixty miles downstream, are upwards of a hundred feet thick.

Gold was first discovered in Colorado in 1858 near the northeast end of the Mineral Belt. The big stampede didn't get underway until the next year. Hundreds of rugged miles separated the discovery areas from the Animas River in the southern part of the San Juan Mountains. Yet by the summer of 1860 a small party led by a man named Charles Baker had pushed into the glacial cup now known as Baker's Park, site of Silverton. What took Baker almost to the outer edge of the Mineral Belt is unknown.

San Miguel, too, was part of his vocabulary. In a letter written in October 1860, to a friend, he stated that some of his followers had scattered out to see how far the riches extended. One goal was the "San Meguil," as Baker spelled the word.

San Miguel is, obviously, a Spanish name. Spanish records show that traders out of New Mexico, in search of furs and deer hides, had reached the San Juan Mountains by 1765. One of those traders, Andrés Muñiz, acted as guide for Fray Silvestre Vélez de Escalante and Fray Francisco Domínguez in 1776, during their fruitless search for a usable trail between Santa Fe, New Mexico, and Monterey, California. The explorers crossed the San Miguel in August of that year—but recorded it as the San Pedro, the name Muñiz used.

The name San Miguel appeared years later out of nowhere. Presumably the change was the work of Hispanic traders who intermittently followed the Escalante-Domínguez trail as far as the vicinity of the Great Salt Lake while questing for pelts and Indian children they could sell into slavery. These Mexican traders blazed the way for American trappers after they had established themselves in Taos, New Mexico, during the 1820s. In the early 1830s one of the Anglos, Antoine Robidoux of St. Louis, built a post near the junction of the Gunnison and Uncompahgre rivers; the town of Delta sprawls there now. The San Miguel is the next stream west of the Uncompahgre. It would be strange indeed if some of the beaver Robidoux acquired before Ute Indians ran him out in 1844 did not come from the willow tangles of San Miguel Park. So, if we could trace Baker's steps before 1860, we might well learn that he had heard of the San Miguel from some veteran mountain man who, in his turn, had worked a way into the region along trails shown him by Hispanic traders from New Mexico.

Did the detachment from Baker's party on the Animas reach the San Miguel? Frank Hall says, in volume four, page 317, of his *History of the State of Colorado*, published in 1895, that they did. Following the lead of a Lieutenant Howard, the men presumably worked their way north between the colorful walls of Mineral Creek, which joins the Animas in Baker's Park, turned northwest along Bear Creek (now known as the South Fork of Mineral), and from its headwaters crossed Ophir Pass into what became known, in the lieutenant's honor, as Howard's Fork, a branch of the San Miguel's South Fork.

Moreover, says historian Hall, the town of Howardsville, a few miles above Silverton and for a brief time the county seat of San Juan County, was also named for the lieutenant.

Where Hall unearthed this information is unknown. No one has been able to find out who Lt. Howard was or whether he even existed. Howardsville was not founded for more than a decade after he had left Baker's Park—if he was ever in it. As for Howard's Fork of the South Fork of the San Miguel River, well, that name evidently also just floated airily in from sources that cannot now be traced. Too bad. It would be interesting to discover the true Howards, for they were the pioneers. They were the first Americans of the industrial era to reach the region's outer edge. What were they like?

In the fall of 1861, after a year of unprofitable mining, winter quarrels, summer recriminations, and a growing fear of Indians, the group that had followed Baker's trail to the Animas River disintegrated. Because of the economic doldrums that gripped Colorado, partly as a result of the Civil War, further prospecting in the San Juans languished. Changed conditions, however, soon sent new stirrings through the Mineral Belt. Silver was discovered in large enough quantities to take some of the magic away from gold; Nathaniel Hill learned how to smelt refractory ore; and in 1870–71 railroads bloomed along Colorado's eastern slope. Sources of supply no longer seemed hopelessly remote. Soon, optimists said, rails and smelters would penetrate the mountains. Investors would follow, and mining would surge as vigorously as it was then surging at the fabled Comstock Lode in Nevada.

Simultaneously reports came in of a rich strike at what was called the Little Giant Mine near Baker's Park. Dozens, then scores, then hundreds of prospectors hurried there. To avoid the long journey through northern New Mexico that the Baker people had followed, most of the newcomers struck straight for the Rio Grande in San Luis Valley. They followed it to its headwaters. Hacking out trails barely fit for burros, they crossed the Continental Divide at either Stony Pass (12,588 feet above sea level) or at Cunningham Pass,

steeper but somewhat lower (12,090 feet). During the next couple of years, it is said, two thousand men staked out more than one thousand claims in the mountains around what became the town of Silverton.

They had no legal right to be there. In 1868 chiefs of the various Ute tribes had signed a treaty with the United States that gave them, as a reservation, about one-quarter of western Colorado. Because of the way the Colorado Mineral Belt slanted, most of the mining districts lay safely east of the reservation's boundary line, in white hands. Not so the San Juans. Those mountains reared up barely west of the boundary and, in Indian eyes, were sacrosanct.

Though the Indians threatened incoming parties, they were restrained by Ouray and other chiefs from launching full-scale attacks. The chiefs meanwhile fired off eloquent protests to every federal agency they supposed might have authority in the matter. President Grant's notoriously corrupt Indian Bureau responded with ineffective noises. Depending on which history you read, the War Department did or did not order troops into the area to drive off the miners. It doesn't matter; the outcome in all disputes over Indian land had been preordained long before this country won its independence. The miners raised the standard howls of outrage. Were honest taxpayers to be shot by unwashed savages? Were enlightened progress and economic well-being for all Colorado to be halted so a handful of nonproductive Indians could keep on chasing deer through the valleys? But in this case at least there was no bloodshed. A commission was appointed to make yet another treaty with the Utes. Headed by Felix Brunot, a truly compassionate man and friend of the Indians, the group dealt patiently and, for those times, fairly with the tribe. They would buy the mountains from the Indians, paying them a perpetual annuity of $25,000 a year, mostly in the form of goods. Recognizing inevitability when they saw it, the Utes capitulated and on September 13, 1873, ceded four million acres of the San Juan Range to the United States.

Old ranch buildings, Deep Creek Mesa

The way was open now for miners to go freely into any or all of the mountain valleys that radiated like spokes out from the highland hubs of the range, notably the Red Mountain district, primary sightseeing target of today's Million Dollar Highway between Ouray and Silverton. Of many difficult trails, those leading into San Miguel Park were the worst. One was the route Lt. Howard reputedly had blazed over Ophir Pass; a traveler could then follow the Howard Fork to the San Miguel's South Fork, the South Fork to the main stream, and turn east into the cul-de-sac. Another way was to push up the main stem of Mineral Creek to the vicinity of Red Mountain and then strike northwest through alpine swales to Black Bear and Imogene passes, the latter over 13,000 feet high. Or one could do as the early trappers (and Linnard Remine) had probably done: find a way to the Gunnison River and from there skirt the entire northern and part of the western flanks of the great massif, splashing across many lovely streams along the way until reaching San Miguel Canyon, where tall pines stood strong against ledged slopes of the deepest red.

Though prospectors may well have reached the above-timberline basins at the head of the river in 1874 or even earlier, no firm records exist until 1875, when John Fallon strode onto the stage like a one-man show. And yet it is hard to believe he did not have one or more companions. Plenty of associates must have been available in feverish Baker's Park, and what would happen if a lone man broke a leg in those formidable wastelands, got blood poisoning from an infected cut, or was struck by lightning, a real possibility during the high country's almost daily late-summer thunderstorms? Besides there are indefinite but nagging references to a man named White. Fallon, though, is the one who went back to Silverton in October with a long list of claims to record, none of which mentioned a sharer.*

---

*Silverton, founded in 1874, quickly supplanted Howardsville as the seat of La Plata County, and retained the honor when San Juan County was split away from La Plata in 1876. A little later Ouray County absorbed the northern part of San Juan County. By law, mining claims had to be recorded at whatever county seat held jurisdiction over the area embracing the discovery. The frequent shiftings of county seats during the second half of the 1870s, together with the careless way with which the record books were sometimes handled, lends a certain piquancy to the hunt for historical beginnings.

First, however, another lesson in geography, this one dealing with the high basins and cirques that rumple the great watershed curve enclosing the upper San Miguel. Begin with Cornet Creek, which drops into San Miguel Park via a tightly enclosed little waterfall. At the head of Cornet Creek is St. Sophia Ridge, a spectacular line of weather-fractured pinnacles running from northwest to southeast. Extending outward from the ridge is a twin-pointed peak now called Mendota, 13,220 feet in elevation. It is a key spot. Southeast of it is a series of basins shaped like giant scoops. They are called, in geographic order, Marshall, Middle, and finally Savage Basin, all drained by branches of Marshall Creek. Due south of Savage Basin, beyond a formidable ridge 13,000 feet high is Ingram Basin, source of the spectacular waterfall at the very head of San Miguel Park.

In late July or August John Fallon, either alone or in company, made his way into Marshall Basin. There he followed a prominent vein northwest until it splintered against the steep slopes of Mendota Peak. He called the twin-tipped summit Ansborough or Ausborough Peak—the penmanship in the old record books is not distinct. On its sides he filed five claims, the Emerald, Tripple, Sheridan, Ansborough, and Fallon. (Since he named the Fallon for himself, might the Ansborough have been named for a companion? And what of the Marshall for whom the basin was named? There is no record of anyone named Marshall at all, unless he was part of the Tripple.) Of the five claims, the Sheridan is the one to remember.

By law no claim could be more than 1,500 feet long and 300 feet wide, or 10.33 acres. The law also required that the claimant sink a discovery shaft on his claim. Some prospector shafts were pretty shallow, and that is probably true of Fallon's. The one he (and his companions, if any) worked hardest on was the Sheridan. With reason, for showy ore lay almost at the grass roots. Not wanting to return to Silverton empty-handed, the prospector(s) carefully sorted out and broke into manageable pieces as much of the best ore as his small train of donkeys could carry. Legend insists that when Fallon reached town in October, he received $10,000 for his harvest.

One of the earliest views of Telluride (no telephone poles are visible yet), the San Miguel River, and the mouth of Bear Creek Canyon.
Denver Public Library Western History Department

San Miguel City, pictured in this early view from George Crofutt's Grip-Sack Guide of Colorado, attracted more interest than embryonic Telluride because of nearby placer diggings.

Miners pose for their pictures beside the Smuggler-Union's Bullion Tunnel, about 1900—just before Telluride's labor strife erupted.

The stratigraphy of precious metals: on top are the mines that feed ore and clutter to mills located as far up the San Miguel Valley as possible. Just downstream is the little mill town of Pandora. Still lower, where the valley widens is the supply and commercial center of Telluride. Denver Public Library Western History Department

Scant time was wasted on early construction projects, as witness the plank sidewalks and protruding wooden signs. Burros (donkeys) were the omnipresent delivery vehicles. Denver Public Library Western History Department

Haskell, now disappeared, was a resting place for Dave Wood's freight wagons and stagecoaches bound for Telluride and Rico. Colorado Historical Society

A mule train heads for the peaks with timbers for some mine. Note that mules are led (and ridden) whereas donkeys are driven. Denver Public Library Western History Department

An epic packing feat was Dave Wood's transporting nearly a mile of unbroken
tram cable to a high-altitude mine by winding it into coils and hanging one coil to
each side of a mule—a whole string of carefully placed mules.

So he must have been feeling good on the morning of October 7, 1875, when he picked up a pen in the county recorder's office and filled out the standard form which began,

> Know all men by these presents, That I the undersigned have located and claimed, and by these presents do locate and claim, by right of discovery and location, in compliance with the mining acts of Congress approved May 10th, 1872 . . .

One form per claim, each containing as accurate a description of the property's location as could be made without actual surveying. John Fallon alone signed each form, lending credence to the story that he had done the work alone, unless he had bought out his helpers with his share of the $10,000.

Jump now to mid-July 1876. Three men, J. F. Gundaker, John Summa, and J. B. Ingram walked or rode from Silverton into Marshall Basin, perhaps because they had heard of Fallon's strike. They, too, staked out claims on what they called Ansborough Mountain. And they spent considerable time looking over the Sheridan and also the Union, a property that had been staked to the southeast of it, on the same vein.

Later Ingram told this story. He and his companions stepped off the length of both the Sheridan and Union claims and found that each exceeded by five hundred feet the length allowed by law. It seems strange that experienced miners who knew that exact surveys would eventually have to be run would make such a mistake. But, says Ingram, they did, and so he, Gundaker, and Summa, after determining where the claims should have ended, were able to insert a thousand feet of their own in the gap. In high glee they named the intrusion the Smuggler.

There's another story. This one says that an associate of Fallon's in 1875, a man named White, had staked out for himself extensions to the Sheridan but had not been able to complete the assessment work required by law. One implication is that somehow Ingram knew White would not be able to finish the process. Accordingly the Ingram trio hurried up to Marshall Basin, found the claim and jumped it. Later Ingram invented the excess-length story to take away the odium of his act. There is no way of knowing now which story is true.

From Marshall Basin the three wandered south to the deep gorge at the head of the San Miguel River. There they located what they called the Broken Hatchet Lode. In the process Ingram also nailed down another small claim to immortality by giving his name to the gulch and the dazzling waterfall that drains it.

In the late 1870s, the upper San Miguel district was as tough a place to work a mine as any in the United States. The lodes with the greatest promise stood 11,000 or more feet above sea level. Snow limited operations to five or six months a year. The quickest way to get ore to an efficient smelter in Denver was to pack it over Imogene Pass to Ouray on burros and transfer it to ox-drawn wagons for the 120-mile trip to the Denver & Rio Grande railhead, which by then had reached Alamosa in the San Luis Valley. Freight and smelter charges ran well over $100 a ton. The reverse problem—getting timber, coal, mining tools, and supplies back up the hill to the workers—was almost as costly. Waiting for the smelter to pay for the mineral it had extracted was another drag.

The only way to overcome the obstacles was to hand sort every rock that came out of the diggings. Men who knew ore eyeballed every piece. Those that looked rich were tossed onto a pile for shipment; lesser pieces were put aside for handling after costs had dropped. Waste was chucked onto the dump. The quantity of waste far outran that of ore, for the drifts and shafts that followed the stringers of mineral—stringers only inches wide in places—had to be big enough to let miners work in them.

Ingram persisted. According to Frank Fossett, a journalist who made a living by writing books puffing Colorado's principal gold and silver camps, the owner of the Smuggler (his partners are no longer mentioned) in 1879 shipped fifteen tons of handpicked ore whose value averaged from $470 to $530 a ton.

By contrast, Fallon found the burden at the Sheridan more than he had anticipated. In 1878 he leased the mine to William Everett and J. T. Donnellan, the latter of whom, it will be recalled, was one of the new commissioners of the town of Columbia. By employing almost as many sorters as miners the lessees produced eighteen tons, but the value, said Fossett, was slightly less than that of the Smuggler's fifteen tons.

In view of those picayune figures it is not surprising that both Fossett and a competitor, George A. Crofutt, author of the popular *Grip-Sack Guide of Colorado*, chose to concentrate on the San Miguel placer mines—at the Montana, just below Columbia, which slid its gravel down steep chutes to the river for washing, and the Keystone, below San Miguel City, for instance. By 1879 the Keystone had installed a huge hydraulic monitor, in effect a sort of water cannon, and was relentlessly undercutting and caving down a long gravel bank 150 feet high. The debris made a mess of the river, but Frank Fossett didn't consider this worth mentioning. Excitedly he declared that the immense deposits, like those of California, were attracting the attention of capitalists, "and it is safe to say that in a few years the yield of gold dust will be enormous." To which Crofutt added an ebullient amen: "This country is *surely* destined to become the most important placer mining portions of the state, if not of the world." But Crofutt did recognize one drawback; there was far more gravel in the valley than water for washing it, especially in late summer and fall. "Could any process be discovered, whereby placer ground could be worked successfully *without* water or with very little . . . this country would yield untold millions."

Meanwhile Columbia was advancing snail-paced toward its goal of becoming a wide-awake city capable of controlling the economic and political future of the region. One necessary step was sending the results of the election of July 13, 1878, authorizing incorporation, from the county seat at Ouray to the state capital at Denver and from there to the General Land Office and the Post Office Department in Washington, D.C.

Now comes a small mystery that has troubled local history for a century. The Postal Department declined to authorize a station called Columbia. The common explanation is that there was a Columbia in California and that unsurmountable confusion would result from the letter-writing public's generally slipshod penmanship; state abbreviations then in use (Cal for California and Col for Colorado) would be indistinguishable. *However*, there was a Placerville in California, but this duplication had not prevented the establishment of a post office at Placerville, Colorado, sixteen miles downriver from Columbia. And after the postmaster general had denied the name Newport to the little settlement near the mouth of Marshall Creek, the petitioners had suggested Folsom after one of the owners of a nearby mine. That name was allowed at the very time Columbia was being rejected, although there is also a Folsom in California.

Some unsung genius—there is absolutely no record of how this came about—broke the impasse by proposing the name Telluride for the city in the middle of San Miguel Park. Whoever made the suggestion was evidently the victim of a mistake.

Telluride is an ore of the nonmetallic element tellurium in combination with a high percentage of gold and a considerably lesser percentage of silver. Telluride ore looks much like pyrites—fool's gold—but is softer and responds quite differently to blowtorch tests. An amateur prospector without a blowtorch might easily identify worthless pyrites as telluride and leap to entrancing conclusions. For instance, there had been something of a rush a few years earlier to a supposed deposit of telluride near Boulder, Colorado. Apparently similar misidentifications had taken place in or near San Miguel Park. Actually there is little or no telluride in the area. Nevertheless, someone who thought so, or perhaps wanted others to think so, suggested the name Telluride for the town earlier voted to be Columbia. The postmaster general agreed, and on July 26, 1880, assigned a post office named Telluride to the site occupied by Columbia. Certainly Telluride was the more marketable name of the two.

Now the confusion deepens. On August 17, 1880, three weeks after the assignment, the post office of Telluride was transferred to the town of Folsom, originally Newport. Why? Local shenanigans for economic benefit? Confusion in Washington over the simultaneous applications for name changes? Who straightened out Telluride's identity is unknown, but on December 13, 1880, the post office, Telluride, was returned to its original location, although the town itself still clung to the name Columbia.

Town and county records remain silent about all this. Perhaps the commissioners were more worried about confusions in property rights than about malfunctioning mail service. For during the shifting of names, the General Land Office had assigned townsite rights to an entity called Columbia. Titles to the town's real estate now had a firm source, and real estate was beginning to move. Town lots were being surveyed along every street. Twenty-six buildings were up and there would have been more if the sawmill at the mouth of Bear Creek, across the river from the southeast edge of town, had been able to turn out more lumber. What kind of title mix-ups would occur if the town changed its name to fit the post office? The orderly way would be for the post office to fit the town. Under the circumstances the town council decided not to rock the boat until someone came up with a workable solution.

CHAPTER THREE • **PLODDING ALONG**

In May 1881, prospector A. W. Dillon endeavored to bring his wife up to date on affairs in San Miguel Park:

The town here is called Columbia but the post office is Telluride. Below here two miles is the old [five years old!] town of San Miguel, but it is about dead. All of the people are leaving and coming to Columbia.

As for Newport, having been denied that name and having lost its brief hold on the post office called Telluride, it was absorbed by Pandora, an increasingly vigorous adjunct to the mills at the foot of Marshall Creek. In short, Telluride/Columbia rose to be the queen city of San Miguel Park while still suffering from an acute case of mixed identity. Even the newspapers across the mountains in the county seat of Ouray didn't know what to call it. On June 21, 1881, the *Solid Muldoon* reported that every available lot in Telluride [sic] had been filed on and that the town already supported seven saloons and a dance hall. A month later the same paper described a foot race for "$500 a side" in Columbia [sic]. No wonder outsiders were confused.

Regardless of name, the town was in dire need of a road into its cul-de-sac. Unable to finance a thoroughfare out of public funds, Ouray County resorted to a toll road. Several groups were given franchises to build segments of the long stretch over Dallas Divide to Placerville and on up the San Miguel River to the town. Recompense would come from charges the builders could then levy on every man, wagon, and beast that used the highway.

The work of the ill-financed contractors turned out to be little better than no road at all. Protests mounted until the beleaguered county turned to Otto Mears, a pint-sized, heavily whiskered, Russian-born orphan who, after fighting with the California Volunteers during the Civil War, had turned his hand to keeping store and trading with the Utes in the San Luis Valley. Soon realizing that western Colorado's greatest need was decent transportation and that he could exact high tolls for providing it, Mears plunged into a construction program that earned him the title of "The Pathfinder of the San Juans." Early in February 1881, he took over the Ouray franchises of his predecessors with the proviso that he build a first-class highway not just to "the Miguel," but on through Ophir and over Lizard Head Pass to the booming town of Rico on the Dolores River.

Wildflowers near Dallas Divide

The frenzy at Rico was probably what persuaded him to undertake the project. In 1879, while the Rico district was still part of Ouray County, fantastic strikes of silver led a reporter from the Ouray *Times* into flights of fancy; "All are as wild as March hares. . . . This place impresses one as having gotten here before it was sent for . . . wine and women, cards and caterers, houses and horses, men and burros, money and mines, storms and stores. . . . "

Thus lured, Mears followed the retreating snow line of spring with a hundred or so Mexican laborers and ten big freight wagons loaded with plows, and axes, picks, and shovels. By September 23, 1881, he had reached Telluride/Columbia. As far as Keystone Hill, the *Solid Muldoon* said, there wasn't a grade that a horse couldn't travel along at a steady trot. Nor was that all. The building of the road prompted a group of entrepreneurs to string a telegraph line beside it to Ouray, there to hook onto another line that skip-by-hop eventually reached Denver.

Neither telegraph nor road, which outsiders regarded as a mere branch of the main stem to Rico, dispelled San Miguel Park's sense of isolation. Reaching the county seat to attend to essential business still took more time than lawyers and busy merchants liked to spend. When they did make legitimate complaints about the way things were run, they were ignored. What they needed, there at the outer edge, was a county of their own and the advantages this would offer to local politicians.

The splitting of Dolores County away from Ouray County on February 19, 1881, with Rico as county seat, stirred the malcontents to emulation. Maneuverings in Denver produced results; early in 1883 the legislature split Ouray County again, creating San Miguel County, whose boundaries ran from the river's towering eastern watershed to the Utah line. Only the eastern tip had any population to speak of. The same legislative act designated Telluride, *not* Columbia, as the governing seat of the new entity. But the plat of the town that had been sent to the General Land Office in Washington as a first step toward obtaining title to the townsite's 78.57 acres

gave the name Columbia to the very same spot. In 1882, moreover, the town's mayor, Charles F. Painter, had gone all the way to the Lake City branch of the General Land Office and had given the clerk full payment of $98.21 ($1.25 an acre) for the ground on which Columbia stood. The next and final step would be issuance of a patent by the President of the United States to the city of Columbia, *not* to Telluride. Until that happened no individual titles to real estate within the town would be secure. Accordingly there was no hurry on the part of the commissioners to confuse the slow-moving bureaucratic process by introducing a second name.

On April 3, 1883, the commissioners of the new county gathered in a room above Hurley's Corner Saloon to hold their first official meeting. As mayor, Charles Painter had no business there. As county clerk, he did. He kept the minutes of the meeting and during that first session referred to the town as Columbia, followed by Telluride in parenthesis . Soon, however, he settled on the unadorned name Telluride, though he was the one who had paid out, as town trustee, $98.21 for a place called Columbia. As county clerk he also kept a record of all land transfers, especially mining claims, in a large gray book.

A curious statistic is connected with his name. Ten months before that first meeting, when he was twenty-six years old, he had married twenty-one-year-old, German-born Eliese Rowher. Their first child, Estelle, born just before the April meeting, is said to have been the second child born in Columbia/Telluride. This record, if accurate, bespeaks a considerable dearth of marriageable women of child-bearing age during the first five years of the town's existence. The pace quickened in '83, however, perhaps because political independence lured in a more stable population. According to the marriage book still resting in the county courthouse, eight couples were wed that year.

But if births were rare before 1883, school-age children, apparently brought to Telluride by their parents, were not. In 1883 thirty-seven such youngsters were running around, too many to be taught in private homes, as had been done since the establishment of a school district in 1881. So one of Painter's first acts as county clerk was to record the purchase by the town of two lots, on which a wooden schoolhouse was built at a cost of $3,000. Replaced later by brick, the building now houses the town hall; the old school bell on the town hall roof is now the fire alarm bell.

In 1885 the United States government finally granted a townsite patent to Columbia, *not* Telluride. Titles thus being confirmed, the county commissioners decided to build a permanent courthouse at the southeast corner of Fir Street and Colorado Avenue. They moved into the two-story brick building in February, 1886. On March 9, 1887, fire gutted the structure.

This disastrous end to permanency allowed the commissioners to remedy a mistake. The old building had faced north, so that throughout the winter the front offices had been shadowed. Perching the replacement on the high, north side of the avenue would not only bathe its front in light but would also allow the government center to visually dominate most of the central part of the town. With that in mind, they purchased new lots at the northwest corner of Colorado Avenue and Oak Street, a block from the old location. Their logical bit of solar engineering was followed ever afterwards by whatever businesses—the Sheridan Hotel, the banks, and so on—wanted to emphasize their prosperity.

The purchase of the lots involved the commissioners, for the second time, in the annoyances faced by residents who bought local real estate—straightening out property rights in a place that had two names. There were other exasperations. It was difficult to explain to business and family correspondents that mail intended for residents of Columbia should be addressed to Telluride. A number wrote Columbia regardless, and no doubt some of their letters went astray to Columbia, California. The misdirection is commonly given as the reasons for the town's decision to at last change its legal name to Telluride, but a more compelling motive was ending the civic schizophrenia.

On May 5, 1887, petitions signed by a majority of the town's taxpayers were presented to the town's board of trustees. The board agreed, and on June 4 both of the city's newspapers carried announcements that there really was a Telluride, a name no other American village bore. A distinctive place: there was some pride in that.

The new courthouse cost $9,415. This figure included $425 for tearing down the old jail—a stone structure twenty by twenty feet, with slit windows in walls two feet thick and eleven high—and moving it stone by stone to its proper place beside the new courthouse. If Butch Cassidy, Tom and Bill McCarty, and Matt Werner had been caught after robbing the San Miguel Valley Bank of a little more than $20,000 on July 24, 1889, that stone building is where they would have been lodged. But if they had been caught, their careers might have ended then and there, and Telluride would have lost one of its well-ballyhooed claims to fame.

The whole courthouse setup can be viewed symbolically. It is a rather handsome building, two stories high, narrow, and built of red brick designed to echo the red slopes of the valley that rise steeply three blocks to the north. It is trimmed with white and topped with a pyramidal tower in which the commissioners thoughtfully ordered a new fire alarm bell to be placed. Its sturdiness, conservatism, and yet fundamental optimism—built twice within little more than a year—reflect the qualities of the town that surrounded it at the time of its construction.

Telluride never had a wild boom of the sort that put Rico and any number of other sudden mining camps into overnight frenzies. As late as 1900, according to the *Telluride Journal*, it had had no lynchings, one big robbery, and "only two or three murders." A quiet, orderly place. Like Iowa. But distance, altitude, forbidding topography, and lack of transporation were not like Iowa, and kept all but a small handful of investors away. With few exceptions, to be noted shortly, the high-altitude mines had to develop slowly and carefully, as their own finances allowed.

During the 1880s, two properties, the Smuggler and the Sheridan, were primarily responsible for such prosperity as the town had. J. B. Ingram and his associates kept on working the Smuggler as they always had. The Sheridan's career was more checkered. Originally, it will be recalled, its discoverer, John Fallon, had leased it to John Donnellan and William Everett. Then in 1880 he sold it to investors from Milwaukee, the first outsiders to show interest in San Miguel lode mines. After struggling with the property for two years, they announced it was open for sale. Somehow word floated across the Pacific to a mining engineer named J. H. Ernest Waters. Waters had roamed the San Juans on consulting jobs during the late 1870s and early 1880s before accepting a position with the Chinese government as advisor in mining matters. Aware of the Sheridan's potentials, he sought out British and Scottish investors in the Orient, raised $250,000, hurried to Telluride, and closed the deal. No doubt he paid himself a hefty commission and, in addition, was hired as manager of the new company.

He followed Fallon's custom of leasing operations while keeping an eye on the whole Marshall Basin scene. A property that quickly caught his attention was the adjoining Mendota workings, owned by John Donnellan and William Everett. The pair had lost their lease when Fallon had sold the Sheridan to the Milwaukee group. Concentrating on their own diggings, they had put the Mendota into sparkling shape. After considerable dickering, Waters bought it for his firm. The price is not known, but it was enough to let Donnellan and Everett shake the snow of the San Juans from their boots and become, in the words of the *Telluride Journal*, "landlords and realty holders in Salt Lake and Denver."

The main reason for the Sheridan's and the Smuggler's increasing profitability was the slow approach of better transportation facilities. In 1882 the narrow-gauge Denver & Rio Grande Railroad reached both Silverton to the southeast of Telluride and Montrose to the north. Silverton was closer, about twenty miles from Telluride as compared to sixty-five for Montrose. Reaching Silverton, however, required crossing passes more than 13,000 feet high, an impossibility in winter. But there was a new smelter in Durango, some forty-five miles by rail from Silverton, and that enabled the Marshall

Basin mines to get quick returns on their ore—high-grade ore because donkeys did the packing to Silverton and holding down volume was imperative. Each summer upwards of six hundred of the nimble-footed little animals carried ore out of the basin and brought back as many sacks of coal as they could in order to avoid empty pack saddles on the return.

All other ore went by wagon down along the San Miguel River to Placerville and from there over Dallas Divide to the now-vanished freight and stage stop of Dallas, located beside the Uncompahgre River about two miles north of present-day Ridgway. There the Telluride-Rico road hooked onto the highway running between the railhead at Montrose and Ouray. Montrose to Dallas, Dallas to the San Miguel—two sides of a right triangle. The roundabout journey jarred the economic sensibilities of Dave Wood, a freighter already on his way to becoming a San Juan legend.

To shorten the distance, and to keep from paying tolls to Otto Mears, Wood built a shortcut from Montrose directly southwest to a point near Placerville, where he joined the Telluride highway. The work cost $15,000 but saved fifteen miles, a full day's haul for freight teams and three hours for each stagecoach. Wood called the road, and others he built, the Magnolia Route—I don't know why—and painted the name in huge letters on the tarpaulins that covered his loaded wagons.

In early days he often used oxen as draft animals, as many as twenty yoke (forty animals) to a wagon that was hauling heavy machinery. A common sight in the towns was a long line of them lying down under their yokes in the middle of the street, chewing their cuds while the wagons were unloaded at some store or warehouse. They were big wagons, eighteen feet long and six deep. Generally a trailer was hitched on behind. Several of the double-jointed contraptions made up a train. A special herder (more than one if the train was large) watched the oxen as they grazed at night, brought them in at dawn, helped with the hitching, and caught what sleep he could during the day on top of one of the jolting vehicles.

As roads improved and demands for speed quickened, Wood switched to mules. He hauled everything: the personal possessions and furniture of families moving into or out of Telluride, groceries, ore, coal, fireworks for the Fourth of July, big spools of cable, coops full of chickens, barrels full of beer, grindstones, and cookstoves. In winter he used sleds. Nevertheless, storms sooner or later blocked him. On such occasions he received desperate pleas: "Our ore house is loaded. A delay in shipment will mean we'll have to borrow money to pay our bills—and we have $40,000 worth of ore on hand." Hurry! Always hurry! While the passes were closed, goods piled up at the warehouses. When finally his shovelers cleared the block-ades, he attacked the clots of merchandise with what looked like frantic disorganization but never was.

On reaching Telluride, the consignments were sorted and supplies for the mines were shifted to long packtrains of mules and jacks. There was heavy human traffic as well, particularly on Saturdays and Sundays. By the early 1880s the mining companies had managed to build enough shelter to keep operating all winter. Hundreds of men lived in bunkhouses and ate well in the boarding-houses. (Good food helped reduce turnover.) They worked ten-hour shifts, day or night. At the close of the Saturday day shift, workers who were free could go to town, if they wished, and enjoy Telluride's numerous and obliging fleshpots. Orders for riding horses were sent to the packers, who led the saddled animals up on that day's trip. The miners whipped the rented mounts back down the hill at a faster pace than was always safe. Late on Sunday they rode back with their hangovers. Dismounting at the mines, each turned his horse around, looped the reins over the saddlehorn and gave the beast a slap on the rump. The self-returning taxis, knowing what this was all about, made beelines for the warm barns at home.

These hundreds upon hundreds of head of livestock consumed prodigious amounts of hay. Ranchers sprang up on every grassy, aspen-shaded mesa. Hay was constantly being hauled to the livery stables in town and barns at the mines. The removal of manure was a monumental problem, not always successfully coped with. Clouds of flies hovered over the town's warehouse district and, to the exas-peration of housewives, buzzed out into the residential sections.

But even as the jam seemed to be growing hopeless, new devel-opments took place that promised better times, both financially and domestically.

CHAPTER FOUR · **THE BEGINNINGS OF THE BOOM**

In 1887, the Denver & Rio Grande Railroad reached Ouray and then sat there as if it had reached track's end. This brought Otto Mears onto the scene. He was currently building a short line between Red Mountain and Silverton to act as a feeder for the D&RG stub that ran up along the Animas River from Durango. Now he saw a chance to spin out a truly noteworthy line. He'd begin ten miles below Ouray at a junction he called Ridgway and go through Rico to Durango—172 miles, counting a branch of six and a half miles to Telluride and Pandora. He called the chimera the Rio Grande Southern and financed its building by selling several million dollars' worth of first mortgage bonds, mostly to the D&RG, which of course would benefit from his labors.

Construction began in the spring of 1890. Fifteen hundred workers, scattered out in widely separated camps, drove the main line from Ridgway over Dallas Divide and up the San Miguel River to its South Fork. He kinked a way over the cliff at the head of the Fork by means of the fabled Ophir Loop, and crawled on past Lizard Head Pass to the Dolores River and Rico. The Telluride branch left the South Fork at a place called Vance Junction and doubled back on itself for a rush at Keystone Hill, which it ascended by means of a stiff, 4-percent grade on the opposite side of the river from the wagon road. Rails reached Telluride on November 23, 1890; the first train chuffed in three days later. Thanksgiving! Yells, toasts, booms of blasting powder. Tootling mightily was the Telluride Cornet Band, well-named considering Cornet Creek as well as the number of cornets in the ensemble.

Nearly a year later, on October 15, 1891, the band played at another celebration, this one designed to extol, at Rico, the joining of the north and south sections of the road. Unhappily, the southside track layers failed to complete their work on time. The festivities went on regardless, for elaborate plans had been made. Otto Mears, accompanied by the governor of the state and various political, railroad, and commercial bigwigs, arrived by special train from the north. More than three hundred celebrants from Telluride filled eight coaches of their own, five pulled by one diminutive locomotive and three by another, for a single narrow-gauge engine could not pull many cars up the twisting Ophir Loop. Several dignitaries tapped somewhat ineptly at the symbolic silver spike, even though, as events turned out, the actual connection was not made until December 19. After a stupefying feast and endless redundant toasts at the Enterprise Hotel, those still awake danced until the approach of dawn.

San Miguel County Courthouse, Telluride

During the railroad years, two other industrial innovations—electric motors and aerial tramways—reached Telluride. Motors were brought in by Lucien L. Nunn. He was small as Otto Mears, fully as ambitious, and much better educated, having drifted in and out of colleges and law schools in both the United States and Europe. Footloose, he followed the Colorado mining excitement to Leadville, where he went broke attempting to develop a first-class restaurant. Moving on to Durango, Nunn launched a more modest eatery and, in his spare time, built shacks that he rented to the stampeders who had followed the D&RG into town. Still dissatisfied, he and a friend walked north through Silverton and over the high passes to Telluride. He was about thirty when he arrived.

Tireless, he took jobs as a carpenter, invested his earnings in more shacks, read omnivorously, and began practicing law. He was a spellbinder, and his rise was meteoric. In 1888 he bought control of the San Miguel County Bank, which Butch Cassidy's bunch would rob the next year, and turned from building shacks to erecting commercial "blocks" on Colorado Avenue, renting store space in them at what were then exorbitant rates.

He soon realized, from loans his bank made to mines and mills, that the major problem facing them was the high cost of power for driving machinery. Steam was fine, but fuel had to be packed to the boilers, and after nearby supplies of wood had been consumed, coal had to be imported at costs ranging up to fifty dollars a ton. Air could be compressed in surface plants and piped inside the mines to run hoists and rock drills, but distance was limited.

Electricity tantalized. Men had known for years that the energy of swiftly flowing water could be transformed by a dynamo or turbine into electrical energy and that this energy, after coursing through a wire, could turn a motor or produce illumination. During the 1880s Thomas Edison had solved enough of the technical kinks of direct-current transmission to light street lamps and turn wheels in a few nearby plants. As the last year of the decade rolled around, Telluride entrepreneur J. H. Ernest Waters, of the expanding Sheridan Mine,

and a few associates built a small direct-current generator for brightening the principal street corners and saloons. Across the divide on the Ouray side, the Virginius Mine, was putting in another direct-current plant in an effort to reduce its energy bills.

Nunn, ever alert, knew of these things when he went East and to England on a business trip in the winter of 1889-90. It is likely that he also knew direct-current electricity is prohibitively expensive to transmit over long distances. While he was in the East, he also learned that George Westinghouse, working with patents obtained from William Stanley and Nikola Tesla, was about to challenge Edison with generators and inductive motors capable of utilizing alternating-current electricity. Its voltage, unlike that of direct current, could be stepped up high enough by transformers to force it long distances over relatively thin copper wire. In other words, alternating current would be much cheaper than direct, if it worked as well under rugged field conditions as in Westinghouse's laboratories.

These things were in Nunn's mind when he stopped off in St. Louis, on his way back to Telluride, to meet with the principal stockholders of the Gold King Mine and its nearby mill, which were located near the high Alta Lakes between Telluride and Ophir. The remote property was heavily in debt to Nunn's bank. As he went over the books with the nervous stockholders, he noticed how much the manager of the mill and the mine was paying to have coal packed in.

Inspiration struck. About two and a half miles down the steep mountainside from the Gold King, the Howard and Lake tributaries of the San Miguel's South Fork roared down the cliffs toward each other in a dazzling foam. Nunn had already obtained generous water rights on both streams, intending to use the liquid for working hydraulic placer mines stretching along the main San Miguel from the foot of Keystone Hill. He could turn some of that water into a generator of alternating current, and if it worked . . .

Uneasily perched the man who rode an ore bucket on a tramway. Modern ski lifts borrowed the tram's techniques, but improved on comfort and safety.

John Grimsby

The mine buildings, boardinghouses, shops, snowsheds, and waste dumps of the fabulous Tomboy Mine were crowded close together in Savage Basin, 11,000 feet above sea level.

Denver Public Library Western History Department

Russian-born Otto Mears built many of the first wagon roads and narrow-gauge|railroads in the San Juan Mountains. His greatest construction feat was also Telluride's economic salvation—the Rio Grande Southern.
Denver Public Library Western History Department

The Rio Grande Southern, Rico-bound from Telluride, posed for a picture beside famed Lizard Head Peak. Denver Public Library Western History Department

Ames had a short life as a mining town, but achieved lasting fame when lawyer L.L. Nunn placed his epochal power-generating station nearby in order to electrify the Gold King Mine 2.6 miles up the mountainside.
Denver Public Library Western History Department

The New Sheridan's uninspired architecture did not keep it from being the town's favorite hostelry. The adjacent building was later burned to the ground and never replaced. Colorado Historical Society

A brass band, a hose cart, flags and a troop of mounted men introduce another of Telluride's famed Fourth of July celebrations, this one in 1887. Colorado Historical Society

Providing hay for the animals that worked above and underground launched the first ranching enterprises in the mountains. Colorado Historical Society

Fast life in the Cosmopolitan Club. Deer heads above the bar, a roulette table, a painting of a nude, a shoeshine boy, and an amiable marshal—what more could a relaxing miner want?

He told the stockholders of his plan. Gratefully—they had been expecting foreclosure—they appointed him general manager of the mine. On returning to the mountains, he selected a site for the generating station close to a ditch already prepared for the hydraulic operations and then told his surveyors to locate a route for a power line to the Gold King. Not until then did he get around to requesting his brother Paul, by letter, to visit Westinghouse and familiarize himself with alternating-current generators and induction motors. Paul's engineering experience was limited to what he had picked up teaching science in high school laboratories.

Luck! Lucien Nunn managed the Gold King the way Waters managed the Sheridan group of mines. He leased the property. Straightaway the lessees hit a rich streak of gold. The royalties they turned back to Nunn, plus a donation from Westinghouse, paid the costs of the electric system. Paul proved to have an aptitude for a kind of work which at that date lay outside everyone's experience. He insulated the generator at Ames, the railroad stop near the plant, by setting it on oak blocks over which melted paraffin had been run at 200 degrees for twenty-four hours. The switchboard was also made of oak impregnated with paraffin, a good thing, too, for when the circuit was broken, as it sometimes had to be, arcs six feet long leaped across the room.

Apprehensively, on June 21, 1891, the Nunns turned a powerful jet of water against a big pelton wheel belted to the generator. The wheel jumped alive, the lights went on in the station, wires hummed, and the engineer in charge of the motor at the mine, 2.6 miles away, telephoned down that the motor was turning, too, in perfect synchronization with the generator. Thus was achieved the world's first long-distance transmission of alternating-current electricity.*

Curiously, L. L. Nunn's biggest problem was realizing the true potential of what he had developed. At first he threw the power system into the pot as one of the secondary assets of the San Miguel Consolidated Mining Company, incorporated for $15 million, which he was putting together to buy both lode mines (he picked up the Gold King for $300,000) and a thousand acres of placer ground along the San Miguel River. Although Benjamin Butler, doddering Civil War general and one-time governor of Massachusetts, agreed to act as figurehead president of the company, many people suspected it of being a swindle. The Ouray *Solid Muldoon* sneered at its general manager, salary $15,000 a year, as "Little Lying Nunn" and said, inaccurately, he "came to Telluride as a dishwasher and his smoothness may in a measure be attributed to the grease he absorbed."

One of the mines Nunn bought as part of the consolidation, the Champion, lay in Bear Creek Canyon, which opens into the San Miguel River just above Telluride. In order to electrify it, he ran a power line from Ames along the hillside above the town. Scenting more opportunity, he bought some vacant lots and erected poles as if intending to invade the territory of the local direct-current company. Bamboozled by his bluff, they switched over to his services.

From all sides mines began clamoring for power. When the ore in the misnamed Champion proved too lean to be mined profitably, inspiration sparked again. Nunn withdrew his system from the San Miguel Consolidated Group and incorporated it as the Telluride Power Transmission Company. Soon his lines were running into the high basins and on across Imogene Pass, 13,000 feet high, to the Camp Bird and other mines on the Ouray side of the divide. It was the beginning, for both Paul and Lucien, of brilliant careers that culminated in the giant Niagara works at Ontario, Canada. By contrast, it is mildly interesting to note, the San Miguel Consolidated placer mines never came close to paying back the sums that were invested in them.

---

*The Ames power plant was just barely the first. Two months later the Lauffen-Frankfort system in Germany came on line—and it transmitted power one hundred miles.

Another engineering marvel of the period was the aerial tramway, developed, as far as Telluride was concerned, in Marshall Basin, where several uncoordinated groups were tearing away at the same massive vein. The first to tackle the transportation problems involved was the Sheridan. After having acquired the Mendota, it reached downhill to absorb the Pandora and Oriental lodes and the forty-stamp mill which those two holdings owned in the little town of Pandora, Telluride's eastern suburb, so to speak.

The next step was getting ore to the mill. To do this the company built a surface tramway consisting of parallel sets of rails for carrying two ore cars hooked to either end of a long cable. As the car loaded with ore descended to the mill, it pulled its empty twin back up to the mine. In that terrain the contraption did not work very fast or very well, but it was enough better than burros that for a time it was rented by the adjoining Smuggler-Union mines.

The arrangement ended when John Porter, president of a smelter in Durango, put together a syndicate that acquired, for $400,000, both the Sheridan group and the Smuggler-Union. (Ernest Waters, erstwhile manager of the Sheridan group, had supervised construction of the Durango smelter for Porter several years before.) In 1890 the arrival of the Rio Grande Southern in Telluride and the government's silver purchasing program, which raised the price of the white metal from 87 cents to $1.05 an ounce, spurred Porter to buy the '76 and the Bullion mines. Both were located on the same massive veins as the syndicate's Smuggler-Union and Sheridan-Mendota holdings. He then added two mines on an intersecting vein, the Emerald and the Pennsylvania.

Porter incorporated the new holdings under the name Smuggler-Union—it would soon be known throughout the mining world—and prepared to work the once-separate properties through a single tunnel that punched into the vein through the Bullion. Volume instantly exceeded the capacity of the two-car surface tram. Accordingly the company built an aerial tramway from the mouth of the Bullion adit to the Pandora mill. Tall wooden towers supported a pair of stationary cables. Small wheels from which ore buckets of a five-cubic-yard capacity were suspended ran along these cables.

Motion was provided by a moving cable to which the buckets were attached by toggle clamps; this allowed the buckets to be detached from the cable for loading at the mine's ore bins and for dumping at the mill. Gravity pulled the loaded buckets downhill. That force, increased first by a steam-driven motor at the mine and then by electricity from Nunn's generating plant, pulled the empties (actually they were generally loaded with supplies and sometimes with men hitching rides) back up the hill.

It was a marvelous way to leap cliffs and chasms, to sail over trees and scree slopes—just as ski lifts, their ultimate descendants, do today. It shook up the ranchers on the mesas by reducing the number of horses, mules, and burros needed for transport, and hence the amount of hay. So the ranchers turned to livestock, and that was the beginning of extensive summer grazing in the San Miguel Mountains. As winter approached, the herds were trailed down to the low country.

For a while it seemed as though Porter's rapid expansion had been a mistake. Ore values in the main vein shrank. Almost simultaneously the government ended its silver buying. Prices crashed—one more element in the bleak, nationwide depression that began in 1893. Telluride staggered with the other mining towns throughout the Mineral Belt. But the local managers soon shook off their panic. Although they had been emphasizing silver, as the rest of the state's mines did, they had known all along that their ores had been sweetened with dustings of gold. Catching their breath, they altered their procedures to concentrate on the yellow metal, whose value, once all impurities had been removed, stayed fixed at $20.67 an ounce.

More luck. Almost at once, miners picked up a handsome streak of gold in the Bullion. Word of what had happened reached Colonel Thomas Livermore of Boston, who had made an enormous fortune in copper mines around Lake Superior and in Montana. He formed a syndicate called the New England Exploration Company and in April 1898 bought the Smuggler-Union, whose name was retained. Guesses on the price range from $3 million to $8 million. Ill-fated Arthur Collins, of whom we will hear more, was named general manager. Under his supervision the tramway was rebuilt and a large mill was added to the already existing facilities at Pandora.

More bonanzas were opened on either side of Marshall Basin. Northwest, at the head of Cornet Creek, was the Liberty Bell. Discovered in 1876 by W. L. Cornett, it attracted scant attention until gold seekers extended its drifts in 1894. Glittering ore brought in outside capitalists who took over, built a tall mill beside the river half a mile above Telluride, and connected it to the mine with a tramway two miles long.

Southeast of Marshall was Savage Basin, named for Charles Savage, who during the late 1870s had staked out lode and placer claims through the high country. His Belmont claim and a few others had been worked sporadically ever since, but to little avail. In 1894, a group of local men, spurred by reports of gold ore in the claims, bought them for $100,000 and consolidated them under the name Tomboy. Between January 1895, and November 1896, they took out $1,250,000, half of which was clear profit. The next year the Tomboy was purchased by the London Exploration Company (i.e., the Rothschilds) for $2 million. By the end of the century it was well on its way to becoming what has been called, with a touch of hyperbole, "one of the great gold mines of the world."

That trio of mines—the Liberty Bell, the Smuggler-Union, and the Tomboy—one per basin—took out close to $2 million in 1899, a time when a dollar amounted to something. Because of them, and also, let it be said, because of several smaller mines at work in the district, Telluride joined Cripple Creek and, to a lesser extent, Ouray as the only bright mining spots in Colorado during those depressed years.

All told, there was reason for optimism as the twentieth century opened.

Powerhouse at Bridal Veil Falls

CHAPTER FIVE • **HIGH LIVING**

Robert Livermore, son of Colonel Thomas Livermore, said matter-of-factly in his memoirs, "Life in Telluride was seldom humdrum." Writer Theodora Kroeber (*Ishi In Two Worlds*) was less restrained:

In that thin, dry air, life moved at a pace of almost terrible intensity—the galloping brevity of spring and summer, the long months of winter with the threat of tragedy always hovering near. Colors were high—the reds in the soil, the fall gold of the aspens, the indescribable sky. Riding in summer and tobagganing in winter were fast and dangerous. One went about totally sensitized. God was a pagan god, in the air, over the mountains, in the waterfalls. But how can I give the feeling-tone of that high Alpine valley, which simply is one of the most beautiful spots in the world?

Fine horses abounded in the town and were the chief conveyances to sumptuous picnics at some high overlook or beside one of the few streams not befouled by tailings from the mines. They served on long pack trips designed to show visitors the remote glories of the San Juans. Men used them to hunt bear, deer, elk, grouse, and ducks. Young women, some of them superb riders, formed riding clubs and went out for gallops on sidesaddles, little

hats pinned on their piled-up hair and the long skirts of their habits streaming out behind. In the winter there was the jingle of sleigh bells. After a big storm, one of the steep side streets was closed for sleds and toboggans that carried muffled young parents, lovers, and children hurtling under the snow-reflected light of the moon.

When horses didn't serve, the little narrow-gauge Rio Grande Southern did. Excursions were frequent—to Trout Lake to fish, boat, or picnic; to root for the home baseball team, the local boxing hero, or a favorite racehorse when they were matched against their counterparts in neighboring towns.

The railroad also brought in traveling circuses and stage and vaudeville shows. The circuses pitched their tents on a meadow near the lower edge of the town. The shows of the 1890s and early 1900s presented their offerings in a loft above Stubbs and Jakway's lumber warehouse. Later the loft was replaced by the Opera House, nestled against the side of the then-elegant Sheridan Hotel. (The source of that name is obvious.) The theater's second-floor auditorium, which may never have served up a real opera, was small but contained the standard appurtenances—box seats, a proscenium ringed with electric lights, a painted, roll-up curtain. It also had seats that could be slid under the stage to make room for formal dances—men in white ties, women in long white gloves and long skirts billowing over a multitude of petticoats.

The great events of the year came on the Fourth of July. The morning began with a parade—the Cornet Band, the fire company's hose carts harnessed to volunteer firemen dressed in tights and ready to race to the nearest hydrants (as they would do later in the day), fraternal orders in uniform, princesses on wagons festooned with evergreens, crepe paper, and blue-and-white columbines. Dogs and firecrackers. Skittish horses.

After the parade, tug-of-war teams from the different mines tried to drag each other through mud holes. Hose teams endeavored to blast each other into submission with heads of water that had dropped almost from the peaktops. Most popular were the rock-drilling contests, on which many miners bet more of their wages than they could afford. The race was against time: who could drill the deepest hole in fifteen minutes? One by one pairs of drillers took position on a huge block of granite that had been set up in the middle of Colorado Avenue. One knelt, holding the sharpened bit of a piece of drill steel upright against the granite. He would turn this steel just a mite between each mighty sledge-hammer blow delivered by his standing partner. When a bit became dull, the men would switch to another, at the same time changing places with scarcely a break in their rhythm, while the street rang with cheers. In the afternoon came the baseball game, horse races, sometimes a rodeo. And stupendous at night, the great multicolored bloom of fireworks dazzled the sky, prelude to dances at the Opera House, in private homes, at the bordellos on Pacific Street.

Telluride paid more attention to its schools than some mining towns did. In 1895 the trustees issued $24,000 in bonds to build the wide, two-story brick schoolhouse that still dominates the skyline. It contained seven large classrooms, a well-equipped science laboratory, a library of 900 volumes, and two basement playrooms for winter games.

Churches, which were privately supported, were something else. On September 2, 1887, the *Solid Muldoon*, in a put-down of Telluride, boasted, "Ouray has four churches and fourteen saloons. Telluride has ten saloons and plans for a church." True enough. Until well into the 1890s small groups belonging to the same denomination gathered for worship in the courthouse, the old wooden schoolhouse, or wherever else space was available. They either conducted their own services or joyously welcomed visiting ministers from other towns. (There is of course, the obligatory story—every mining town tells it—of the minister or priest who climbed across the snowy passes, hanging to the tail of his donkey, to hold services in one of the combination saloons and gambling halls and who afterwards received a sizable collection from the audience. Telluride adds a small twist. One of its visiting ministers, his gambling-hall sermon finished, sat down at a table and sought to increase his take by bucking the tiger.) Be that as it may, change did not come until the gold strikes of the mid-1890s restored prosperity and the town's population edged above 3,000. The Congregationalists then managed to erect a steepled building. The Catholics followed with a small chapel, but the Methodists didn't realize their goal until after the new century had opened.

How many prostitutes lived in Telluride at its peak? The answer depends on whose account you read. Let's just say there were lots. The hills were full of husky young bachelors who didn't want to wait a long time on the few occasions they reached town. Getting their ashes hauled is what they called it, an etymological curiosity of uncertain origin. One fair ash hauler was so popular she took reservations. Surroundings differed. Some of the whores preferred to work alone in small wooden cabins known as cribs; en masse, they were called the line. If the shade of a crib's front window was up, a prospecting client could look in to assay the wares. If the shade was down, he wandered on.

Other girls liked to work at the dance halls, which had bedrooms attached. Telluride's principal halls were the Silver Belle, White House, Pick and Gad, and the Big Swede's. A customer danced briefly with a flimsily dressed young woman, then took her to the bar and ordered bourbon. He got a shot; she generally asked for a brass check she put in the top of her stocking to cash in later—two-bits a check. Some of the girls, incidentally, only danced, and if an overheated partner got rough about it, he was bounced. In the main, dance-hall orchestras were the last stop for alcoholic musicians. The fact that an orchestra played in a whorehouse was no bar to its playing at more proper parties up on the sunny side of the hill. The bordello bands were the only ones available and it was assumed the ladies at the party wouldn't know where they came from. The ladies obligingly went along with the pretense.

In 1902, San Miguel County financed the building of an improved wagon road from Telluride to Marshall and Savage basins and on to Imogene Pass, some tales insist. Townspeople considered it one of the world's great road building feats. Even Ouray-bound stagecoaches, it is said, used it for a time. Riders who have gone over it more recently in four-wheel-drive vehicles, holding their collective breaths, find this hard to believe.

The road followed Oak Street to the base of the red north hill and swung hard right onto a long diagonal. Turning a corner, it entered ravines, clung to cliffsides, bored through a short tunnel, and, where a wide enough shelf couldn't be blasted through the rock, tiptoed over massive cribworks of timber. It climbed past the mouth of the Bullion Tunnel, whose buildings perched unbelievably on the precipitous hillside, left Marshall Basin to the left, and eventually reached the Tomboy. Its purpose was to hurry along human traffic and the hauling of goods too heavy and bulky to fit into tram buckets, which by that time were serving all the upper-basin mines.

Life in the high country quickly improved for some people. To be sure, the mines had always built steam-heated bunkhouses often equipped with running water, bathtubs, and community rooms for reading and playing cards between shifts. Food in general was good, although a traveling engineer, Thomas A. Rickard, reported the coffee at the Smuggler to be fit more for removing boiler scale than for drinking.

The road's big bonus was enabling young professionals to bring their wives into places where nesting simply was not part of the normal routine. Tiny hamlets appeared near the workings, particularly at the Tomboy, where the land was flatter than at the Smuggler. The shacks were stringently cramped, cooking was difficult at 11,500 feet, and fear of accidents was never far away. But there was a post office at the Smuggler; a school, which functioned only during the summer, at the Tomboy; and small stores, equipped with telephones at both mines. A tennis court, surely the highest in North America, was built at the Tomboy. YMCAs, complete with bowling alleys and pool tables, were established at both places. The Ys also furnished space for religious services. A minister came to the Smuggler from Telluride twice a month, and Mary Mott accompanied him in his wagon, or sleigh at times, with her portable organ. Cornish miners, known throughout the mining country as Cousin Jacks, loved to sing and performed well with hymns. They crowded around Mary's organ in packed rings and lifted their voices for as long as she could stay.

Death was common at the mines and often grisly. At those altitudes pneumonia was nearly one hundred percent fatal for those who contracted it. Men fell down shafts; loose boulders sometimes caved in on them from stope roofs. A driller might set off, in his own face, dynamite that had failed to explode when the preceding shift had fired its rounds. Lightning striking outside the Liberty Bell Mine ran along the car rails and electrocuted three workers deep under the earth. But seldom were disasters as horrifying as the Smuggler-Union fire on November 20, 1901, and the Liberty Bell avalanche of February 28, 1902.

The Smuggler catastrophe resulted when a load of hay burst into flame at the mouth of the Bullion adit and set fire to the adjoining buildings. Drafts sucked flame and smoke into the heavily timbered tunnel. Two trammers driving mules hitched to ore-filled cars cut the animals loose, grabbed their tails, and whipped furiously. One of the stampeding mules burst through the flames. The other died, though somehow its driver crawled free.

The drivers were lucky. Twenty-eight men, some of them would-be rescuers, died of suffocation inside the mine. Most were interred in Telluride at a single service. The Cornish wept as they sang, and most of the town filed by the open graves, dropping in sprigs of evergreen as they passed. A little more than a month later, on Christmas, the same Cornish were singing in the saloons. Passersby who stopped a moment outside the door heard an old favorite of the Cousin Jacks, "While Shepherds Watched Their Flocks."

That winter, 1901-02, was marked by heavy snows. The people at the Liberty Bell expected slides but were not unduly concerned. The mine buildings had been placed on a two-acre flat backed by a scraggly stand of trees that showed no avalanche scars. Far above the trees rose the sawtoothed outline of St. Sophia Ridge. A gulch about twenty feet deep and devoid of vegetation sliced down from the ridge directly toward the mine but veered off to the right. Such slides as had occurred since the opening of the mine followed that gulch with a roar that unsettled those who heard it, but did no damage.

At 7:30 in the morning, February 28, a worker saw a slide break loose up near the ridge. He yelled and pointed. Several people paused to watch the mass plunge toward them. A monstrous slide, it filled the gulch with snow, so that the last half of it did not make the curve but crashed straight ahead into the mine compound. It destroyed the boardinghouse, splintered part of one bunkhouse, and carried away the ore crusher and tram terminal. Those who had been outside watching vanished.

The telephone line stayed up. A call for help went to town, only a mile away by a steep trail. Meanwhile those who had escaped the fury seized steel rods and began probing for bodies, living or dead. Soon they were reinforced by townspeople, two doctors among them. When a prober's rod struck a yielding object, he called out and shovelers ran over. They dug up a few corpses (later it was determined that seven men had been killed but some of the bodies were not found until spring) and eight survivors. Injuries ranged from minor bruises to one whose arm had been torn off and another whose skull was fractured.

About one P.M. a second slide cut loose, followed the track of the first out of the snow-filled gulch and slammed into the rescuers. When the clouds of powdered snow settled, one partially buried, injured man was spotted and pulled loose. No other sign of life showed. Morale was shattered. The foreman ordered the injured men put in shape for evacuation, and the column straggled down the trail toward town.

A third slide, following a completely different path, swept four of the men out of the line. One escaped; three died. All told, sixteen men perished and ten were hurt. Two of the dead were volunteer rescuers. One was ranked with the management level—a twenty-six-year-old assayer. Two had graduated from the Colorado School of Mines the preceding spring and had signed on to pick up some experience. The rest of the victims were laborers. The company sent each of the families $300.

The bunk and boarding houses were rebuilt a little distance away where, again, there were no signs of previous slides. Because it was impractical to move the ore and tram houses, they were reconstructed on their original site and shielded against further damage by a huge timber wall a hundred feet long, fifteen feet high, and twelve feet wide. The space inside was packed solid with earth and rocks.

Later, when the company issued its financial report for the year ending September 20, 1902, it was noted that despite snowslides and rebuilding, the company had handled 67,439 tons of ore at an average net profit of $1.62 a ton.

There were other deaths in the mountains that winter, two from explosions, three from snowslides. Resentment filled the ranks of the laborers. The work they were doing was hard and dangerous—nearly fifty deaths in less than a year—and management did not pay adequately for what it demanded. If the Telluride Miners' Union had its way, however, things would change.

CHAPTER SIX • **MOUNTAIN WARFARE**

On July 28, 1896, the militant Western Federation of Miners granted charter number 63 to the local Telluride union. The step practically guaranteed strife.

Mining had changed radically during the twenty years that followed the discoveries made by such individual frontiersmen and local heros as John Fallon, J. B. Ingram, William Everett, and John Donnellan. They had pursued dreams of independence and well-being into the high basins and had succeeded. But the days of sorting out rich ore by hand and packing it on burros to smelters that would turn it into wealth had quickly passed. The values in most ore were relatively low, and profits could be achieved only by volume production. This meant industrialization—railroads, aerial trams, electric motors, big stamp mills, cyanide plants. Obtaining these called for assembling capital into a corporation and marshalling workers into structured patterns. Who then had first right to the wealth that resulted? The stockholders who risked their dollars and hired the expensive engineers and managers needed for large-scale operations? Or the workers who, giving up the frontier's cherished dream of independence and equality, had little left to offer their employers other than raw, ill-regarded muscle?

Amid these difficult questions, the traumatic effects of the depression of 1893 lingered on. Among the panaceas proposed for economic recovery was bimetallism, the pegging of the price of silver to the price of gold at a ratio of 16 to 1. All sorts of favorable economic adjustments would result, proponents of the plan argued. In Colorado thousands of silver miners would be reemployed. The intense emotionalism that accompanied the issue led the Telluride unionists to call their local chapter the 16-to-1, even though their jobs depended on gold rather than silver.

Another attack on the depression was a widespread lowering of the time spent on the job, which had long ranged from ten to twelve hours a day. Eight hours would be better, it was said. Employers would hire additional laborers to fill the gap; workers would perform better because of the new leisure, and so on. Heeding the arguments, the Colorado Assembly passed a bill in 1899 that decreed an eight-hour day for mine, mill, and smelter workers. Though the Colorado Supreme Court declared the law unconstitutional—it deprived workers of their right to sell their labor under whatever circumstances they saw fit—all the mines (but not the mills) at Telluride except the Smuggler-Union reluctantly introduced the eight-hour day at a wage of three dollars per shift, with a dollar a day deducted for board.

Lewis Mine in Bridal Veil Basin

Arthur Collins, manager of the Smuggler, tried to slide around the issue. He introduced the Cornish system of fathom mining, a fathom being defined, in this case, as a cubic area six feet high, six feet deep, and as wide as the vein. Because the Smuggler vein was unusually wide, a man could not turn out his quota in eight hours, but was not paid his three dollars till the ore in the fathom was removed.

The miners asked the 16-to-1 chapter for help in dealing with Collins. On the grounds that no union had a right to interfere in a company's management of its own property, Collins refused to speak to the delegates. The union responded on May 4, 1901, by calling a strike against the Smuggler. Collins in effect thumbed his nose at them by hiring strikebreakers, called scabs by the union, at exactly the terms the local union had asked on behalf of the Smuggler workers—three dollars a day for an eight-hour shift of straight (not fathom) mining. The message was clear. Unions would not be recognized by management.

Unless the local chapter forced the issue, the union was finished in Telluride. So out with the scabs! Radicals in the 16-to-1, probably acting without the knowledge of the chapter president, Vincent St. John, assembled about 250 men and passed out as many rifles as they could lay hold of. Under cover of the predawn darkness, July 3, they marched quietly up the steep zigzags leading to the Bullion Tunnel. There they took cover behind rocks, machines, and the corners of the mine buildings.

Shortly after dawn the hundred or so men employed in the workings began filing out of the adit, their empty lunch boxes swinging in their hands. A twenty-seven-year-old Finnish striker, John Barthell, stepped out from his cover and yelled an announcement he had no legal authority to make: the scabs were under arrest. A mine guard stationed in the tramway building promptly shot him dead. The strikebreakers rushed for their own arms—management had anticipated the possibility of violence—and sporadic firing continued throughout the day. Two strikebreakers were killed. Three were wounded, one of them the mine superintendent.

Toward evening union president Vincent St. John and the county sheriff arrived on horseback. They arranged a truce: the scabs would lay down their arms on the promise of a safe return to town. Negotiations between St. John and Collins would follow.

As soon as the strikebreakers were unarmed, the union men fell savagely on them, beat up many, and, using their rifles as prods, marched the whole troop over Imogene Pass. There they told them to leave the country and never return to Telluride, where several had families. That message was clear, too. Nonunion workers would not be tolerated in Telluride.

Unable to hire enough nonunion men to keep the Smuggler operating, Arthur Collins capitulated and signed a three-year contract agreeing to recognize the union and employ only union men at three dollars a day for a standard shift. The triumphant men of 16-to-1 buried Barthell in Telluride's Lone Tree Cemetery and marked the grave with an ornate tombstone that can still be seen there. On its base they chiseled words from Longfellow—a prostitution of poetry, fumed mining engineer T. A. Rickard when he passed by shortly afterwards.

> In the world's broad field of battle,
>   In the bivouac of life
> Be not like dumb driven cattle—
>   Be a hero in the strife.

During the following months the union's gestures of defiance increased. After the deadly fire at the Bullion Tunnel in November 1901, the 16-to-1 charged the Smuggler-Union with criminal negligence in not having installed protective doors at the adit. It showed its financial strength by building Telluride's only hospital, with the words *Miners Union* emblazoned over the entry. It sponsored a convention in Telluride at which the locals of all the region's principal camps were consolidated into the San Juan District Miners' Union—a move that led mine owners to organize the San Juan Mine Owners' Association. Business and commercial interests joined the owners with a Citizen's Alliance devoted to the cause of "industrial freedom."

On August 1, 1902, at the invitation of the union, Eugene Debs, presidential candidate of the Socialist Party, which he had helped found, delivered a ringing credo at the Sheridan Opera House. A month later, again at the union's invitation, two top officials of the Western Federation, Edward Boyce and Big Bill Haywood, delivered the oratorical fireworks at the 16-to-1's boisterous Labor Day picnic. They could hardly have infuriated the owners more.

All this was too much for some unbalanced mind. On the cold night of November 19, 1902, a shotgun roared outside the living room window of Arthur Collins's home at Pandora. The buckshot charge smashed through the oak back of the chair in which he was sitting and killed him almost instantly. He left behind a wife and two small children.

The county grand jury issued a total of fifty-seven indictments against Vincent St. John and eight other men. Judge Theron Stevens of the district court and a pioneer resident of Ouray, dismissed them for lack of evidence.

Collins was replaced as manager of the Smuggler by charismatic, controversial Bulkeley Wells. Marvelously handsome with an olive skin, black hair and dark, brooding eyes, Wells could easily have played Rudolph Valentino roles in early movies. He was an expert polo player, a crack shot with any kind of hunting gun, and a gambler with ice water in his veins. He kept himself in perfect physical trim.

Though born in Chicago, he quickly scaled the inner bastions of Boston society. After graduating from Harvard as a mining engineer in 1894, he married exquisitely beautiful Grace Livermore, daughter of millionaire Colonel Thomas Livermore, whose company owned the Smuggler. Impressed by his new son-in-law, the colonel sent Wells to Colorado to look after his widespread western interests. Soon Wells was also investing money in likely mines for another millionaire, Harry Payne Whitney, Jr., of New York.

In Colorado, Wells and his wife divided their time between the rarified society of Denver and Colorado Springs. Denver's social arbiter, Mrs. Crawford (Louise) Hill, was so taken by him that she kept a full-length painting of him on the stair landing in her mansion, where it would greet her every time she went up to bed. But intimate romances, if the Crawford connection really was intimate, were not enough for Bulkeley Wells. Fascinated by uniforms and military authority, he became a captain in the Colorado National Guard. In that capacity he rode with the state militia into Cripple Creek, where labor strife was even bloodier than in Telluride. He carried what he learned with him to Arthur Collins's desk at the Smuggler-Union.

The uneasiness into which the town had been plunged by Collins's assassination was intensified during the spring and summer of 1903 by the deplorable antics of the Colorado Assembly. The state supreme court, it will be recalled, had declared unconstitutional an earlier bill calling for an eight-hour work day. The state's voters retorted by passing, 72,980 to 26,266, a constitutional amendment mandating legislative implementation of a new eight-hour law. Instead of obeying the mandate the assembly let itself be paralyzed by intense lobbying by state corporations and adjourned its 1903 session without taking action on the measure.

Mill and smelter hands who worked long hours at low wages treating Cripple Creek ore at plants just outside Colorado Springs immediately struck. Mine workers at Cripple Creek itself supported them in a sympathy strike. Violence flared and in marched a thousand militiamen, "to do up this damned, anarchistic Federation," as one of the officers put it.

A similar situation developed at Telluride. Although the mines there had won an eight-hour day, mill workers at the Smuggler, Tomboy, Liberty Bell, Nellie, and the rest lacked that benefit. Like their counterparts beside Pikes Peak, they waited patiently for the assembly to act, and when it failed to do so, they walked off their jobs in September 1903. The mines followed, creating a situation of such volatility that Governor Peabody, a rigid conservative, dispatched six railcar loads of state troops to Telluride as requested by the mine owners, to keep order as order was defined by the Mine Owners' Association and the Citizens' Alliance. The owners and their supporters, it should be added, had already hired professional gunmen to keep the strikers at a distance.

It would be redundant to follow the maneuverings of the next fourteen months. Curfews were imposed; gambling halls, saloons, and brothels were closed without recompense to the owners. Idle men, mostly unemployed miners who hung around the soup kitchens maintained by the union, were arrested, put in railroad boxcars, and hauled out of town several score miles and dumped. Strikebreakers were imported to keep the mines and mills open. Whenever the situation began to look tense, potential trouble-makers were popped into a bullpen, an iron-gated stockade erected in the middle of the main street, and then deported. Many of the exiles kept returning, eluding guards stationed at Placerville and at a little fort built of gray pieces of slide rock beside the Imogene Pass Trail—an uncomfortable lookout manned throughout the chill winter by guards hired by the Mine Owners' Association.

Worried by the constant return of angry men, who often were turned loose by writs of habeas corpus almost as soon as they were rearrested, the commander of the militia prevailed on the governor to proclaim martial law. Writs of habeas corpus were then ignored, and the bullpenning and deportation of "vagrants" were speeded up. In February 1904, when things seemed to be cooling off, the troops were withdrawn, and Wells was left in charge of maintaining order. Turmoil seethed again, and the state troops were recalled. More spasms followed, including the physically violent arrests of Big Bill Haywood and other leading union officials who risked coming to Telluride for a showdown. Finally, on November 29, 1904, the Western Federation of Miners, bloody and bowed, ended the strike.

There was a parting shot. On March 2, 1908, nearly four years after the union's surrender, someone placed a time bomb under the bed on the second-floor porch where Bulkeley Wells was sleeping—in Arthur Collins's former house in Pandora. The explosion blew a

huge hole in the porch floor, knocked off part of the porch wall and sent the bed flying to the ground outside. Protected by the mattress and the fur robe he had covered himself with against the cold, Wells was unhurt.

Though detectives foraged busily, no one was ever apprehended. The episode did show, however, that the old sense of community, once so strong in Telluride, had been severely frayed by the years of strife.

These militia men occupied one of the mines during the labor strife of 1901–04. The reader can make up his own explanation for the prostrate figure in the lower left corner of the photo. University of Wyoming

Bulkeley Wells—the romantic, high-living, hard-fighting, union-busting head of the Smuggler-Union Mining Company. Denver Public Library Western History Department

After the bankrupt Rio Grande Southern had ended passenger train service, its place was taken by a hybrid automobile hauling a few passengers and a modicum of freight. Denver Public Library Western History Department

Charles (Buck) Waggoner (left) advertised his bank's stability with photos of stacked dollars, but after the mines had closed, neither picture nor larceny practiced on some of New York's biggest financial institutions could keep his firm afloat. Denver Public Library Western History Department

The empty main street, except for a few autos, shows that the hard times of the late 1920s and 1930s had clamped down on the town with the closing of the mines. Denver Public Library Western History Department

Streets filled with mud by the disastrous Cornet Creek flood of 1914 were washed clear by high-pressure hoses, wielded hydraulic mining style and using water drawn from the same creek's more normal water levels. Homer E. Reid

Until the Black Bear Mine was crushed in March 1925 by an avalanche that killed two people, it furnished ore for the mill and tram house located at the very lip of spectacular Ingram Falls.

A few families and scores of bachelors endured winters at the timberline mines with the help of choral groups, YMCAs, church services by itinerant ministers—and large helpings of patience. John Grimsby

Winter snowstorms like the one that bogged this team in pre-automobile days
brought Telluride new prosperity as a dazzling ski resort.

Wilson Peak and Sunshine Mountain

CHAPTER SEVEN • **SECOND HARVEST**

One tale often told about Bulkeley Wells concerns his inviting favored friends to Telluride and then giving them leases to profitable sections of the mine like a caliph scattering coins. After enjoying Telluride's bright summer days and unrestricted night life while hired miners did the work for them, the lessees returned home $50,000 richer.

There are kernels of truth in the legend. Leasing was a time-honored practice throughout the Colorado mining country. It freed funds and machinery a company manager could use for developing unproved sections of the workings. It also brought income into the company treasury, quite a bit at times, if the leased ground proved rich and royalties soared. In Wells's case there was an additional incentive. Though the strike had ended, animosities ran deep, and he believed workers would perform better for outside bosses than for him. The danger, of course, was that the lessees would tolerate shoddy work while they gutted the mine in order to maximize profits.

How many leases Wells actually negotiated in the years immediately following the strike cannot be determined. Before he abandoned the custom, he made one generous one to a partnership that included his brother-in-law, Robert Livermore, son of Colonel Thomas Livermore. A Harvard graduate like Wells, young Bob had been working at the Camp Bird Mine when the Telluride strikes erupted. To keep in touch with the battle, he occasionally crossed the divide on snowshoes or skis that were long boards with only toe straps as bindings. When the second round of troubles began in 1903, he resigned from the Camp Bird in order to help Wells at the Smuggler. The troubles settled at last, he joined three other men in acquiring a lease.

It was not cheap. They had to buy their contract and then had to equip their workings. Each took a turn managing affairs; the others wandered around enjoying life until the agreed-on rotation brought them, one by one, back underground. The employment gave Livermore knowledge about the Smuggler that would be helpful years later, but the quartet's most significant contribution was the "cleanup"—a sort of second harvest. Their lease allowed them to climb far back into the abandoned Sheridan, where only high-grade ore had been removed during the 1880s. Digging into the loose rock of the old stopes was risky, but they solved the technical problems and reaped well. Naturally, other miners in the area took notice.

Colorado Avenue, Telluride

By then the town had settled down to an era of mostly pleasant living. Though fresh mineral discoveries no longer stirred feverish hopes, still the uninterrupted pounding of the mills farther upstream bespoke steady pay checks for workers and trade for business people. No one seemed to heed the side effects: the wide-open gaming houses and bordellos, the gouged hillsides, or a once-sparkling river turned to a gray sludge by the pulverized and chemically infused rock dumped into it.

The Opera House flourished, especially after it began showing the first flickering motion pictures. The first automobile labored up Keystone Hill, and though everyone was excited, futurologists predicted that because of the area's rough roads and bottomless mudholes, the machines would find only limited use. Horses continued to take miners to work, wagonloads of supplies to their destinations, and picnickers to the flower-strewn mesas.

Formal parties were frequent and gay, none more so than those hosted by Bulkeley Wells at the New Sheridan Hotel. Gossips quickly noticed that his wife Grace and their four children seldom visited Telluride. No one was really surprised when she divorced him in 1918 on the grounds of desertion. Raised eyebrows asked the inevitable question. What had really caused the abandonment? Louise (Mrs. Crawford) Hill? But she did not leave her husband, so that suggestion remains conjecture. What is more certain is that an angry Colonel Livermore withdrew his support from Wells and shortly thereafter put his son Robert in charge of the Smuggler.

Those lovely mountains around the town—it seemed especially shocking when they dealt a haymaker. On September 5, 1909, a cloudburst engulfed the precipitous basin between Yellow Mountain and the flamboyant Vermillion Peaks, turning L. L. Nunn's foresight into a thunderous mockery. Years before, he had sought to guard his Ames power plant against dry summers by damming Hope Lake, high in the basin, and Trout Lake, a couple of miles farther down. The massive runoff from the cloudburst swept away both dams, tore out long sections of flume, and destroyed a dozen miles of wagon road and railroad grades along the main San Miguel.

A saloon keeper who knew a carload of beer consigned to him was due to arrive shortly decided to capitalize on the catastrophe. He sent a long string of pack mules to Placerville, which was as far as trains from Denver could reach, and had them loaded with the stranded kegs. It was almost a parade—two riders in front carrying a banner bearing the sponsor's name. See what Telluride needed first! Tourists since then have been more amused by pictures of the beer parade than the town was at the time.

Nunn's workers got the power plant working by throwing together a patchwork flume and turning every hillside stream into it. Otto Mears was dragged out of retirement to rebuild trestles, bridges, and grades. By concentrating on the Ophir Loop stretch below Trout Lake, he finally got the first Rio Grande Southern train in from Durango on October 25, fifty days after the breaking of the dams. No train came in via Placerville until December 17. Altogether repairs to the railroad cost $314,000, of which $70,000 was paid by Nunn's Western Colorado Power Company because, so the charges went, its dams had been inadequate. What the county spent repairing wagon roads is unknown.

One month less than five years later, at about noon on August 5, 1914, another cloudburst laced with sizzling lightning bolts hit Cornet Creek Basin back of the Liberty Bell Mine. Picking up the waste dump—thousands of tons of stone and pulverized rock—the dark gray wall of water jetted far out over Cornet Creek Falls and mowed down the trees in its path. Totally bewildered by the appalling noise, mothers rushed out into the deluge, screaming for their children.

To make room for expansion, the town council years before had turned Cornet Creek from its normal course by a small dam. Now, seeking its natural channel, the flood leaped the obstruction in a residential section and spread wide, tilting, twisting, and smashing homes. It dropped huge boulders in yards and alleys, filled the lower floors of both the Miners Union Hospital and the Sheridan Hotel with goo, and left five-foot mats of tangled debris in the central parts of Columbia and Colorado avenues. Amazingly, the only person to die was a woman who was pinned against the side of a house and smothered in mud.

The cleanup was fast, for this was a mining town. Boulders were broken into manageable size by dynamite charges so skillfully handled that few windows even cracked. Mud was washed by fire hoses into quickly constructed sluice boxes that carried it to the river.

Between 1905 and 1911, the Telluride district turned out $16,234,038 in gold and silver; the Liberty Bell, Smuggler-Union, and the Tomboy accounted for 90 percent of the sum. After that peak record, production declined, slowly at first and then, during the first World War, precipitously. Chemicals were in short supply; laborers left to work in war industries or join the armed forces. The price of explosives, machinery, freight and smelter services soared, while the value of gold remained fixed by law. Peace brought a brief upswing, but it did not last. Once-productive veins were mined out, and one by one the town's chief workings shut down. The Smuggler-Union, tightly managed by Robert Livermore, went last, in 1928.

Bulkeley Wells's decline was as disastrous as the miners'. He lost his shirt in a radium adventure near the Colorado-Utah border, and still more endeavoring to reopen the fabled Comstock Lode in Nevada. Along the way he married a devoted and gorgeous platinum blonde. At that, Mrs. Crawford Hill reportedly took down his picture from her stair landing and persuaded the Whitneys to stop backing him. His pride broken by failure and debt, he committed suicide in San Francisco on May 24, 1931. He was fifty-nine years old.

Telluride residents clung on for a while through "cleanup leases" that gave people willing to work hard for small returns the right to scavange the old workings. One example concerns two brothers who were anxious to get funds for finishing their college educations. They bought permission to invade the old Columbia mill near the Tomboy. They then spent two summers sweeping the floors, scraping out the old ball and stamp mills, burrowing underneath the bins. By processing the grit and sand they harvested, they earned enough to emerge from Colorado State University with degrees in electrical engineering.

Harry Johnson and a handful of Scandinavian colleagues had a less happy experience. In 1925 they obtained a cleanup lease on the Black Bear Mine, 12,000 feet high in Imogene Basin. Their idea was to go back into old stopes, as Livermore had in the Sheridan, and mine out roofs and pillars left by the original operators. They repatched the buildings, opened the tunnels, and got the tram working again. On March 21, after they had shipped a few freight cars of ore, nine of the workers rode the tram to Pandora for a brief rest. Johnson and six others stayed at the workings. At two o'clock in the morning an avalanche demolished the place. Two men crawled out of the debris relatively unhurt. One way and another, they found and dug out three more—Harry was one—and put some warmth back in their chilled bodies by stowing them between mattresses like the filling of a sandwich. Two others, the twenty-six-year-old cook and her husband, the blacksmith, were parts of a different sandwich. The impact of the slide had carried their bed up against the roof and had crushed them. Their arms were still around each other. They may not have even awaked.

Bootlegging was safer. Colorado went dry before the rest of the nation. Enforcement was lax, and the interim gave time for practice. The stone brewery below town kept right on churning out suds. Stills popped up in every side gulch. It would seem the moonshiners worked cooperatively. Anyway, they produced an extraordinary volume of the fiery stuff. Furthermore, old timers declare nostalgically, it was *good*. They shipped their choicest batches as far away as New York City; Al Capone bought quantities, and private clubs in Denver served it proudly. Ouray patriots make the same claims for their product. So do Leadville survivors. Anyway, the mountain dew helped the mining towns survive—and they certainly needed help.

Charles Waggoner, president of Telluride's one remaining bank, brought a bit of pride to his fellow citizens by figuring out how to use secret bank codes for swindling the biggest financial institutions in New York City out of half a million dollars. He eventually got caught, though, (this was in the fall of 1929) and his bank was padlocked. That left San Miguel County without a single place to make a deposit or borrow a dollar.

In 1931, the Rio Grande Southern quit running passenger trains, substituting in their stead automobiles rebuilt to run on rails. The hybrids were called, derisively, the Galloping Geese. Six or seven passengers could ride up front with the driver; the awkward-looking vans in the rear could carry a sizable clutch of mail and parcels. The last Goose died in 1949. Freight trains ran a while longer, but finally lost out, in 1951, to competition by trucks.

The second World War, which raised the price of lead, zinc, and copper, led two gargantuan companies to plunge back into the horseshoe of peaks cupping the upper San Miguel. One was Telluride Mines, Incorporated, which pulled together into a unit the dozens of claims once embraced by the Liberty Bell, Smuggler, Tomboy, and Argentine. The other large-scale producer was the Idarado, composed of a multitude of lesser known claims acquired jointly by the Sunshine Mines of Wallace, Idaho, and the potent Newmont Mining Company of everywhere. The name Idarado was obviously a compression of Idaho and Colorado.

Though Newmont soon bought Sunshine's share in the venture, it retained the name Idarado and added another with suggestive connotations, the Treasury Tunnel. Idarado's plan was to push the Treasury Tunnel due west from a point beside the Million Dollar Highway as it climbs toward Red Mountain Pass. The ambitious bore would punch under the headwall of the valley into the bowels of the Black Bear, where Harry Johnson's cleanup attempts had ended in tragedy.

Funds for both the Telluride Mines, Incorporated, and the Treasury Tunnel were provided by the Metals Reserve Company, a creation of the War Production Board. The magnitude of the effort that resulted far exceeded anything Telluride had experienced before. Then peace came and prices sagged again, dragging down with them the will to keep on digging. At that critical juncture, Fred Searles of Newmont sized up the situation and decided that a truly massive output could still achieve a black balance sheet. So he acquired Telluride Mines and attacked the entire upper end of the basin with hundreds of miles of tunnels, drifts, adits, stopes, and winzes. Closing the Red Mountain side of the operations and using the best technological know-how available in the mining world, he began pushing upwards of 400,000 tons of ore a year through a new mill at Pandora.

Prodigious amounts of waste accompanied the operation, but the law no longer allowed the slimy discards to be dumped into the river. Instead, they were diverted into an enormous tailings pond between Telluride and Pandora, where huge rainbird nozzles sprinkled it every day to settle dust and to coax a thin cover of specially developed wheat to grow on its flanks. For the first time in nearly a century, the San Miguel River runs clear again.

Mining was back—or was it? By the 1960s a mere handful of men was producing more tonnage than hundreds of miners had during Telluride's heyday. If the town was to be anything but a withering appendage to a vast industrial process busily engaged in exhausting its own resources, some new forms of livelihood would have to be found.

Mine ruins, Savage Basin

CHAPTER EIGHT · **THE ULTIMATE RESORT?**

Bill Mahoney, miner, skier, and developer, tells a tale of strange affinities that can serve as a metaphor for Telluride's long attempt to escape almost total dependence on a single uncertain resource. Back before refrigeration was commonplace, cattle were butchered close to town and, in summer, distributed quickly among the town's meat markets. On occasion, Mahoney relates, a luckless steer or two would be driven up the long road to the mines, killed and skinned. The miners at the Smuggler's Cimarron level, where Bill was then working, would appropriate the wet hide and spread it out beneath a drift face where ore was rich and a blast was due. When broken rock rained down from the explosion, bits of gold popped off the stone and clung to the fresh hide, out of the muck where it was easily recovered.

A potentially superlative recreational hide spreads its skirts, figuratively speaking, around Telluride. The fact was noted as early as the beginning of the 1880s when George Crofutt declared in his *Grip-Sack Guide of Colorado*, "To those desiring to climb the most rugged mountains, visit wild, dismal, and almost impenetrable canyons and 'drink in' the grandest of all American Alpine scenery, and all within a day's ramble from a comfortable hotel, we should certainly recommend a visit to Telluride." The Rio Grande Southern made access to the 'drinking in' far easier than it had been in the days of stagecoaches and wagons. And even without the rail-road, excellent trout fishing and elk and deer hunting were readily available.

There was fun in the snow—sleigh rides and, after big storms, nerve-tingling toboggan and sled runs down one of the steep side streets that had been closed to automobile traffic, after autos had begun appearing in Telluride in numbers following the first World War. And there was skiing.

Some skiing was utilitarian, a way for the town's numerous Scandinavians to skim down from the mines for a weekend. But it was a sport, too. Youngsters snowplowed down the hill from the Catholic Church. Or they'd skijor behind automobiles. Then, in 1936 or so, Bruce Palmer arrived from Austria with a knowledge of rope tows and an ability to activate them with a car motor. It was possible after that to get dragged up the slopes at whose foot the town park was later built.

The tow led to the creation of the Ski-Hi Ski Club, dues five dollars a year. The $800 needed to replace the rope each season was raised largely by townspeople selling hamburgers in a hut at the bottom of the run. The big events were grade school, junior high,

Balloon Festival, Telluride

high school, and adult races. The excitement drew contestants from other towns, and so the club moved its tow to longer—1,500 feet—and more challenging slopes in Grizzly Gulch. If you were good enough, you could even follow the swath that had been cleared for the power line and nosedive down it almost onto the rooftops of the town.

So there were plenty of attractions for drawing in the tourists' gold . . . but the tourists didn't come. Residents laid the blame on their situation. They were too far from major centers of population, roads were poor, competition from wealthier, more accessible places was insurmountable. Besides, Telluride's business had always been mining.

The complacency received a rude jolt in 1953, when Telluride Mines shut down prior to its acquisition by Newmont, which at that time was still conducting its Treasury Tunnel operations from the Red Mountain side of the divide. The town, pessimists sighed, was a goner. The Ghost Town Club of Colorado actually made Telluride the destination of frequent excursions. All those boarded-up garages, stables, stores, houses! What was there to do except dig in the town dump for old bottles colored a delicate purple by decades of mountain sunlight? Mournfully the editor of the *Telluride Tribune* pointed to the obvious: "There was a lack of foresight among us in not making Telluride a great tourist attraction to buffer such a blow."

Hindsight about foresight: but what could be done *now*?

Idarado's shift to Pandora helped some. For the rest, Telluride kept on looking wistfully outside. The Navajo Trail, paved shortcut from Phoenix and Los Angeles to Denver and the upper Midwest was being built across northeastern Arizona into southwestern Colorado. Surely a big sign erected just outside Cortez, where Highway 145 split off for Telluride, would lure a few spenders. And it did. Then there was the possibility that a big federal dam might be built on the San Miguel River a few miles below the mouth of the South Fork. A motel and a dude ranch were built in anticipation, but the final ruling on the reservoir was negative and the blues came back.

Two vehicles—jeeps (more properly four-wheel-drive vehicles) and snowmobiles—finally stirred the town into doing rather than just wishing. By 1960 owning a jeep had become a status symbol throughout the mountains. By following abandoned mine and lumber roads every which way, the powerful little vehicles were opening big areas of the backcountry to vacation homes and outdoor recreation. Just pushing the cars goatlike up rocky ledges, through deep streams, and across sidling slopes was exciting in itself. Tour operators in Ouray (which, being on a through highway, caught more traffic than Telluride did) discovered they could make good money by adding a few extra seats to their jeeps and taking tourists on sightseeing trips along old mine roads into the magnificent tundra and peak country above timberline.

The outcome was inevitable: tie the roads together. Civic organizations in both towns put pressure on their county commissioners to invest in high-altitude road repairs. By the mid-sixties four-wheel-drive vehicles could grind and bang up the old stage road past the Smuggler's Bullion Tunnel, where the 16-to-1 unionists had manhandled strikebreakers in 1901, past the ruins of the Tomboy, once rated as one of the world's great gold mines, and on over Imogene Pass to the road that dropped down Canyon Creek into Ouray. A still spookier ride led from Red Mountain to Black Bear Pass, tiptoed across the lip of Ingram Falls, and nearly wrenched the driver's shoulders from his sockets as he zigzagged down through the cold, wind-blown mists of Bridal Veil Falls.

A lot of people who otherwise would never have crossed the mountains first saw Telluride during one of those rides from Ouray. But Telluride wanted a stunt of its own. What emerged was a glorification of autumn, when an electric-blue sky arches over oriental carpets of oak brush broken by masses of golden aspen. "Coloride to Telluride" they called it and gave free trips in jeeps up the Tomboy road. Seven hundred visitors came in 1965. Travel writers took notice and soon so many caravans of four-wheel-drive vehicles were trundling in for the event that the popularity of the Coloride rivaled that of the town's big Fourth of July celebration, which connoisseurs had long considered the best show of its kind in western Colorado.

Racketing snowmobiles carried the allure into winter. Owners formed a club called the Stump Jumpers and put on a January Jamboree that attracted, the first time it was held, more than seventy-five vehicles and a clutch of salesmen anxious to have people try their wares. The main event (there was a class for women as well as for men) was a grueling twelve-mile race from the Ophir highway up to the Alta Lakes, then down the abandoned Boomerang Road—a doozy, that one—to a final churning climb to Campbell Gardens atop the steep hill bordering the town on the south.

That race course cut across the long slopes, alternating forests and meadows creased by little creeks, that slant steeply from the high country down toward the rim of the South Fork. Nature-made ski country, just waiting. Bill Mahoney, young John Stevens, David Farny, and other leaders of the Ski-Hi Ski Club contemplated it with almost painful regularity. How could it be developed? One notion was to tear Telluride down and rebuild it as a Swiss-style winter resort and run gondolas over the hill to the ski slopes. (The destruction wouldn't have been unduly disruptive. In spite of jeep and snowmobile adventurers, who were transient, only 553 people still lived in Telluride, according to the 1970 census.) But creating resorts, to say nothing of ski areas, cost amounts of money that would have made even Bulkeley Wells blanch. There just wasn't that kind of money in all San Miguel County.

Farny, who had moved from Aspen to Telluride with his wife Sherry to open a mountaineering school for young people, Mahoney, Stevens, Jim Gowdy, another Aspen transplant, and some others got hold of a snow cat to haul skiers to the top of potential runs (the cat transported about 150 people during the entire winter of 1970-71). In summer they worked off their energies cutting stubby little runs through the trees. They invited experts in to look over the scene (each came up with a different proposal) and, most important, they began acquiring options to buy ranches that would be embraced by their proposed development.

Misplaced hope? Not really. In those days, the late 1960s and early 1970s, a craze for skiing was running wild through the Rockies. Promoters went among the peaks like old-time mineral prospectors, hunting for rich strikes. One who came to Telluride and immediately grasped its potentials was Joseph T. Zoline of Beverly Hills, who had discovered the magic of ski development at Aspen. You built lifts and runs, at a loss if necessary, to bring people into an area, and then you sold them, at high prices, real estate on which to build winter homes.

Zoline's arrival coincided with an outburst of tensions in Telluride. This was also the era of the wandering hippies, for want of a better word. They, too, heard of Telluride. It was said to be beautiful, cheap to live in, and free from the stifling afflictions of the materialistic world. They began drifting in: long hair, scruffy clothing, beads, and an unabashed love for marijuana in a conservative town long noted for its production and consumption of straight whiskey.

Just how serious the clashes were depends on whose reminiscences you listen to. Certainly there was a lot of shouting. Tired of being harassed by the natives, the newcomers put together what they called "The Slate" and seized political control of the town. Their first act was to fire the marshal who had come to represent, in the more radical minds, the redneck narrowness they resented so passionately. But at the next election the natives were ready. They regained control, but they didn't rehire the marshal.

No one really won or lost. The more outspoken, though not necessarily the more industrious, of the hippies wandered away as effortlessly as they had wandered in, like the floating miners of yore. Those who stayed did so out of love for the area and for the sense of community they felt was attainable if people worked directly and actively, within a broadly based legislative process, to make Telluride the kind of living place they'd hoped to find when first they came. John and Larry Stevens, Telluride-born, college-educated, and young enough to rap with the newcomers (who weren't so new any more), helped form a bridge to the old-timers and pretty soon

Telluride Ski Resort

Bluegrass Festival, Telluride

Chamber music, Telluride Town Park

Ideas Festival, Telluride

people began smiling about the differences that once had seemed so vitriolic. There were more clashes, to be sure—growth against no-growth, environmental tangles, resort building against a more conservatively-based economy—but by then the fevers had faded. Adjustments were possible.

There were hard times for awhile, and that may have been fortunate, as it had been fortunate during the 1880s when Telluride, way out at the edge of nowhere, had developed slowly enough to escape the mistakes of a boom-time mining psychology. Ninety years later, during the 1970s, those who hung on while other ski areas grabbed the spotlight were better able to figure out the directions they hoped their town would take.

One casualty of the long depression was Joe Zoline, who tried to shave corners with his lifts and runs and eventually lost control. His successors had to discard some of his work completely, rebuild much, and take off in new directions. Still, he was the person who had shaken out the kinks and had made the takeoff under the new management possible. It has been mind-boggling. Ultramodern lifts and runs of varying difficulty have proliferated. Two mountain villages have been planted close to the skiing scene. One is Mesa Z, a carefully laid out, almost totally electronic, energy-efficient, environmentally prudent community for 2,000 people being brought into being by Joe's daughter, Pamela Zoline, and her husband, John Lifton. The other is the Telluride Ski Resort Company's ninety-two-acre Mountain Village. Its master plan envisions 1,600 living units, restaurants, an arts and crafts center, conference facilities, and a golf course. The Village and Telluride will be connected by a spectacular $2.5-million cross-country gondola tram capable of making the trip in twelve and a half minutes. Northwest across the canyon, on a mesa where mules once grazed and sheep now hold dominion, is a new airport which may prove as effective in breaking down the town's isolation today as the Rio Grande Southern was nearly a century ago.

One question does haunt the historian. Isn't the new Telluride as dependent on a single industry as the old? The threat showed during the doldrums of the 1970s. A few jeepers or snowmobilers eating lunch at the Roma Cafe or the New Sheridan Hotel just weren't enough. Additional lures to attract off-season visitors had to be found.

The answer has been an extraordinary series of summer festivals. The seed came not from the town itself so much as from private individuals who had ideas they felt could be presented best in the Telluride setting, and the town has been flexible enough to let them try. Two of the oldest presentations are the film festival, ranked now by the *New York Times* as one of the finest and most innovative in the world, and an out-of-this-world jazz festival. The biggest gathering, in terms of attendance, is the bluegrass festival. In between are celebrations of wine, mushrooms, hang-gliding, mountain films, chamber music, dance, and river running. As part of the same spirit, esoteric sports are growing popular—ice climbing, rock climbing that concentrates on solving route problems rather than on reaching the top, heli-skiing, mountain biking and so on, all calling for new philosophies about the relationships between man and nature.

Do these things make a viable town? Or is Telluride just one more glitzy, trendy, sophisticated but essentially unanchored ski village? Some cynics wonder. But John Naisbitt, author of *Megatrends* and part-time resident of Telluride, is wholly upbeat. His festival of ideas is the area's latest and most challenging offering, for he is questioning the whole planet's future. And here, in Telluride, he says, America can glimpse its new direction—replacing ugly, environmentally poisonous, unmanageable urban conglomerations with villages responsive to their citizens' basic desires. No stultifying rusticity is involved. These creative people will stay in contact with the rest of the diversifying world by means of instantaneous communication networks.

A twenty-first century Florence, showing the way to a renaissance? Charlie Painter, who presided over the original town when it rejected the outworn name Columbia for something entirely new, might not find the comparison out of line at all.

ACKNOWLEDGMENTS AND READING LIST

It is not possible for me to acknowledge all those persons whose tales and companionship have given this book such sinews as it has. Many have passed on but should not be omitted for that reason. They include Ed Pierce, who worked in Van Atta's store during the early 1900s; George Belsey, whose father was minister of the Congregational Church during the same period (George put some of his reminiscences on paper; Alta Cassietto loaned me a copy); Theodora Kroeber; Frank Wilson of the Busy Corner Pharmacy; Mr. Segeberg, long-time proprietor of the Sheridan Hotel; L. G. Denison; Homer Reid; Robert Livermore; and of course my own family, from Granddad and Grandmother Painter on to my brother Dwight, who left this scene much too soon.

More recently I have been indebted to Peggy Kanter and the most considerate staff in the San Miguel County Courthouse; to Barbara Cox and Arlene Reid at the county museum; to Bill and Susan Kees; John and Diane Tutt; David and Sherry Farny; Larry Holmgren; John Stevens; Bill Mahoney; Wendy Brooks; my son and daughter-in-law, David G. and Val Lavender; and on and on.

Friends on whose writings I have leaned heavily are Mel Griffiths (*San Juan Country,* Boulder, Colorado, 1984) and Duane Smith (*Colorado Mining,* Albuquerque, 1977; *Song of the Hammer and Drill,* Golden, Colorado, 1982). Smith, in addition, generously cast his knowing eye over this manuscript prior to its publication.

Mostly, though, I am indebted to my wife, Mildred, who not only accompanied me on trips to Telluride but afterwards helped pull the chaos together and then typed the manuscript that resulted.

Except for Richard L. and Suzanne Fetter's *Telluride, from Pick to Powder* (Caldwell, Idaho, 1979), the Telluride story appears in print only in disjointed bits and pieces. The following list represents only a part of the items I consulted. The search began with an investigation of the claim filings and title transfers stored in stacks of dull, gray tomes shelved in the Ouray and San Miguel county courthouses. Particularly useful were the pre-twentieth-century minutes of the meetings of the San Miguel County Board of Commissioners. The vexing problem of the town's dual names gains some light from Alta Cassietto's brief survey and from *Colorado's Postal History* (1971) by William Brown, James Ozment, and John Willard, a book loaned me by Barbara Spencer of Ouray. More data on early times appears in the appropriate chapters in puff books by Frank Fossett (*Colorado,* rev. ed., 1880), George Crofutt's *Grip-Sack Guide of Colorado* (rev. ed., 1885) and Don and Jean Griswold's very useful *Colorado's Century of 'Cities.'*

First-person reminiscences in which Telluride plays a role include Harriet Backus, *Tomboy Bride* (Boulder, Colorado, 1969); T. A. Rickard's *Across the San Juan Mountains* (New York, 1903); L. L. Nunn, *a Memoir* (Ithaca, New York, 1933) by Nunn's long-time friend and employee, Stephen A. Bailey; and Robert Livermore's *Bostonians and Bullion* (Lincoln, Nebraska, 1968). Not a reminiscence, but close to being a first-hand account is Dave Wood's biography, *I Hauled These Mountains in Here,* by Dorothy and Frances Wood (Caldwell, Idaho, 1977). T. Lindsey Baker adds to Bailey's memoir of Nunn with "The Ames Power Plant," *Colorado Municipalities* (Sept./Oct. 1975), as do Inez Hunt and Wanette Draper on pages 57–76 of *Lightning in His Hand, the Life Story of Nikola Tesla* (Hawthorne, California, 1964).

A few specialized studies are Josie Moore Crum, *The Rio Grande Southern Railroad* (Durango, Colorado, 1954); George Suggs, *Colorado's War on Militant Unionism* (Detroit, 1972); Roger N. Williams, *The Great Telluride Strike, 1901–04* (Telluride, Colorado, 1977).

Isolated chapters on Telluride pop up in Wilson Rockwell's *Uncompahgre Country* (Denver, Colorado, 1965); Robert Brown's *Empire of Silver* (Caldwell, Idaho, 1965); Marvin Gregory and P. David Smith, *Mountain Mysteries, The Ouray Odyssey* (Ouray, Colorado, 1984); and Muriel Wolle's *Stampede to Timberline* (Boulder, Colorado, 1949) and its off-beat sequel, *Timberline Tailings* (Chicago, Illinois, 1977).

A scouring of back issues of the State Historical Society's *Colorado Magazine*, of the Denver Westerners' *Brand Book* and the four-volume set, *Pioneers of the San Juan* (Durango, 1942–61) will yield occasional, worthwhile recollections and profiles. Incomplete files of the various Telluride newspapers—the *Journal*, the *San Miguel Examiner*, the *Tribune*, and the *Times*—repose in the State Historical Society, the Western History Department of the Denver Public Library, and, on microfilm, in other depositories in the state's universities. Don't overlook the Ouray *Solid Muldoon*, which at times cast a sardonic eye on Telluride doings. Much can also be gleaned from the picture collections in the San Miguel County Museum, Telluride.

D. L.

Many people contributed generously of their time, information and hospitality while I was photographing *The Telluride Story* this past year. Unfortunately, some of those important names now slip my mind, and to those people I apologize. The ones that I easily recall include Durfee Day, Bill and Susan Kees, John Stevens, John and Diane Tutt, the Telluride Chamber Resort Association, and Christina Watkins. Also, a special thanks to David Lavender, without whose enthusiasm for this book and introduction to the town, this project would have been quite a bit more difficult to initiate, not to mention complete.

G. H.

The Telluride brass band of the early days won prizes throughout the state for its musical prowess. Today the town's jazz festival brings new kudos to the beautifully located, born-again mountain hamlet.

Denver Public Library Western History Department